TWISTED
TRUE TALES
FROM SCIENCE

EXPLOSIVE EXPERIMENTS

TWISTED TRUE TALES FROM SCIENCE

EXPLOSIVE EXPERIMENTS

STEPHANIE BEARCE

Prufrock Press Inc.
Waco, Texas

Library of Congress Cataloging-in-Publication Data

Names: Bearce, Stephanie, author.
Title: Twisted true tales from science : explosive experiments / by Stephanie
 Bearce.
Other titles: Explosive experiments
Description: Waco, Texas : Prufrock Press Inc., [2017] | Audience: Ages 9-12.
 | Includes bibliographical references.
Identifiers: LCCN 2016051030 | ISBN 9781618215765 (pbk.)
Subjects: LCSH: Explosions--Juvenile literature. | Disasters--Juvenile
 literature. | Science--Experiments--Juvenile literature.
Classification: LCC QD516 .B397 2017 | DDC 904--dc23
LC record available at https://lccn.loc.gov/2016051030

Copyright ©2017 Prufrock Press Inc.

Edited by Lacy Compton

Cover and layout design by Raquel Trevino

Image credits: Page 8: Félix León; Page 10: Wisegeek; Page 29: Wikimedia Commons/
Banza52; Page 33: Collier, John, *A Glass of Wine with Caesar Borgia*, 1893; Page 67,
71: Los Alamos National Laboratory Archives; Page 73: Wikimedia Commons/
Mr.98; Page 80: Alan Bean; Page 85: U.S. Air Force; Page 92: Igor Kostin; Page 107:
NASA; Page 123, 126: ESO/M. Kornmesser; Page 128: Maximilien Brice, CERN

ISBN-13: 978-1-61821-576-5

Printed in the United States of America.

At the time of this book's publication, all facts and figures cited are the most current available. All telephone numbers, addresses, and website URLs are accurate
and active. All publications, organizations, websites, and other resources exist as
described in the book, and all have been verified. The author and Prufrock Press Inc.
make no warranty or guarantee concerning the information and materials given out
by organizations or content found at websites, and we are not responsible for any
changes that occur after this book's publication. If you find an error, please contact
Prufrock Press Inc.

Prufrock Press Inc.
P.O. Box 8813
Waco, TX 76714-8813
Phone: (800) 998-2208
Fax: (800) 240-0333
http://www.prufrock.com

TABLE OF Contents

NEW DEVELOPMENTS

EARLY EXPLOSIVES

FIRE POWDER

Chinese Emperor Xianzong of Tang (Li Chun) wanted to live forever. He was convinced that it would be a wonderful gift to his subjects. After all, wasn't he the best ruler that China had ever seen? Of course the people wanted him to rule China for all eternity. Emperor Li Chun ordered his alchemists to get busy and whip up an elixir that would give him life everlasting.

The alchemists got busy mixing every concoction they could think of, from animal dung and willow bark to gold flakes and charcoal. But in 800 AD, Chinese science was a mix of superstition, belief in magic potions, and experimenting with any chemical they could find. And nobody was willing to tell the emperor that an elixir of eternal life was an impossibility. The alchemists knew that would be the end of their own lives. So they kept mixing and testing the potions on the emperor.

> Emperor Li Chun ordered his alchemists to get busy and whip up an elixir that would give him life everlasting.

They were especially fascinated with substances that seemed strange or magical to them. For example, they believed sulfur was an enchanted substance because it was a stone but it could burn. Other rocks were resistant to fire. Mercury was also mystical because it was a metal and yet it was also a liquid. The alchemists were sure that if they mixed these miraculous elements with other chem-

icals, eventually they would find the recipe for eternal life. So they kept mixing, and they kept feeding the elixirs to the emperor.

Unfortunately, the alchemists didn't know that arsenic, lead, and mercury are all poisonous to the human body. The potions gave the emperor bloody gums, vomiting, fevers, and seizures. They also caused him to go insane. The emperor became so demanding and unreasonable that the palace guards assassinated him.

Although the experiments didn't turn out too well for the emperor, the alchemists did make an amazing discovery. During their testing, they came across one combination of elements that had an explosive result. When the alchemists mixed together sulfur, charcoal, and saltpeter, the potion burst into flames, then exploded the entire building where they were working. The alchemists never fed this mixture to the emperor, but this discovery was one of the first times humans

4

experimented with the compound that would someday be known as gunpowder.

The alchemists called the mixture *fire powder* or *fire drug*. As they continued to work with the fire drug, they studied how to control the explosions. They learned that they could mix metal shavings with the powder and create colorful explosions that would light up the night sky. The Chinese became famous for colorful displays of fireworks and used them to celebrate festivals and holidays.

But the Chinese also realized that anything that explodes could be used as a weapon. Military leaders

Although the experiments didn't turn out too well for the emperor, the alchemists did make an amazing discovery.

began using fire powder to frighten their enemies. They packed bamboo tubes with the fire drug and lit each one with a silk fuse. Then they threw the bombs at invading armies. At first, the Chinese just used the noise and explosion of light to frighten their enemies. But then it was discovered that if they put scraps of metal or shards of porcelain in the tube, it would explode and could injure and kill the enemy soldiers.

The Chinese army created fire arrows that could be shot during a war. A lump of fire drug wrapped in paper and sealed with pine resin was attached to the shaft of the arrow. As the archer launched the arrow, the fuse was lit and the arrow rained fire down on the enemy soldiers.

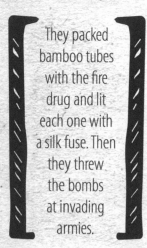

They packed bamboo tubes with the fire drug and lit each one with a silk fuse. Then they threw the bombs at invading armies.

They also used catapults to launch metal balls full of the fire drug and set enemy buildings on fire.

By 1200 AD, the Chinese had made a powder so strong that it could burst an iron case. They built a bomb named the "Heaven-Shaking Thunder Crash Bomb" to fight against the Mongols who invaded their country. The explosion of this bomb could be heard 33 miles away and sent projectiles flying through iron armor.

Next they began experimenting with rockets and learned how to control the burn of the powder enough to launch rockets at their enemies. Eventually they designed "erupters." These were tubes packed with explosive powder and projectiles. They worked much like a cannon, but some were small enough that they could be handled by just one person. These handheld cannons were the very first guns. Larger "erupters" took several men to handle, and they had to be very careful in calculating the right mixture so the cannons didn't explode before they launched. They got creative with what was packed in the cannons. Some of them were filled with pieces of metal, and others shot bundles of arrows. One of their weapons was named the "Nine-Arrow Heart Piercing Magic-Poison Thunderous Fire Erupter."

These weapons were far more sophisticated than anything invented in Europe. During 1200 AD, the French and English were still fighting with broadswords and catapulting stones. It would be more than 100 years before Europeans used the fire drug or gunpowder in their wars.

ROCKET MAN

Chinese legends tell a strange story of the first man to ever test rockets as a form of travel. His name was Wan Hu, and according to the story, he decided to take a trip in a chair powered by fireworks.

Wan Hu supposedly lived in the 1500s in China and had a special chair built and attached to two kites and 47 gunpowder-filled rockets. On the day of his launch into outer space, Wan Hu took his seat and had his servants light the fuses of the rockets. The servants ran as soon as the rockets were lit. There was an enormous explosion. When the smoke and fire cleared, there was a hole in the ground, but Wan Hu and his chair were gone. It was not a successful space launch, but it did demonstrate the power of gunpowder.

FOR THE LOVE OF SALTPETER

When the Europeans learned about the explosive properties of gunpowder, they were hooked. By the 1300s, Spanish, French, and British kings were experimenting with gunpowder, learning how to use it in weapons and for construction. Before the invention of gunpowder, the only way to remove or crush large rocks was with manual labor. Gunpowder was valuable not only because it could be used to fight

Before the invention of gunpowder, the only way to remove or crush large rocks was with manual labor.

against enemies, but also because it could blow a big hole in the Earth. Miners and builders could see amazing opportunities for gunpowder. There was just one problem. Saltpeter was hard to find.

The first two ingredients for gunpowder—sulfur and charcoal—were fairly easy to obtain. Sulfur was a mineral deposit found near ancient volcanoes. It could be mined or dug out of the Earth. People had been making charcoal for centuries by burning wood in kilns to remove the moisture from wood.

But saltpeter was a mysterious substance. People called it Chinese snow because it was white in color and about the consistency of snow, and the Chinese introduced its usefulness to the world. But nobody was really sure how to make it. They knew that it

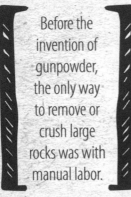

seemed to "grow" on rock walls, in some caves, and on top of animal dung. They also knew that it was the main ingredient in gunpowder. A whopping 75% of gunpowder is saltpeter. Without saltpeter, there is no big bang.

The rulers of Europe were desperate to get their hands on as much saltpeter as they could. When it was discovered that saltpeter could be found on the dirt floors of barns and in homes, the kings issued warrants that gave some of their assistants the authority to go to farms, dig up the floors of the barns, and take the saltpeter. These men became known as "petermen," and they were hated as much as tax collectors.

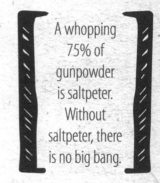

A whopping 75% of gunpowder is saltpeter. Without saltpeter, there is no big bang.

The petermen could dig up the soil of any place where they found saltpeter. They ransacked houses and tore up the floorboards of churches. If saltpeter was found, they took it, but the poor landowners received no compensation.

Some farmers and businessmen decided to take matters into their own hands and learned how to make saltpeter grow. They dug trenches and filled them with all the animal and human manure they could find. They also added scraps of food or rotting plants. As the dung mixture decomposed, it formed saltpeter, or potassium nitrate crystals. The crystals were scraped off and sold. It was a smelly and disgusting job, but it was profitable. The saltpeter farmers just had to be careful that the petermen did not learn what they were doing. Many of the farmers paid bribes to the petermen. The petermen were happy with this. They got money without having to dig through the manure piles.

Saltpeter was also found in caves where bats had lived and produced centuries of bat poop, or guano. Islands where there were deep deposits of bird poop were also mined for saltpeter. When saltpeter was discovered in India, the British government quickly decided that it would take India as one of its colonies. The saltpeter mines supplied the British for decades.

Supplies of saltpeter were critical during wartime. The colonists had to buy saltpeter from the French when they were fighting the American

Revolution, and during the Civil War, blockades of saltpeter shipments depleted the arsenals of the South.

In 1910, two German scientists, Fritz Haber and Carl Bosch, invented a way to take nitrogen from the air. This eliminated the need for saltpeter farms and changed the way the world used nitrogen.

EAT YOUR SALTPETER

Eating something that is made from animal manure sounds disgusting. But in the Middle Ages, people were desperate to find ways to preserve meat. There was no refrigeration, so meat could not be stored. After a few days, it went rancid and became infested with maggots. Then somebody got the idea of experimenting with rubbing meat with saltpeter. The nitrites that are found in saltpeter act as a preservative. So in the Middle Ages, people began rubbing their meat with a mixture of salt and saltpeter and then hanging it up to dry or smoking it—something that led to eventual practices of using straight nitrites for curing meat we eat today, like cold cuts and hot dogs.

KING EDWARD'S EXPERIMENT

It was a bloody battle. King Edward III had 10,000 archers shooting arrows at the French army. But the French were 60,000 strong. The French knew they could defeat the pesky English invaders. They had more men and more horses. It would certainly be a French victory, and the vulgar English would run back home to their island where they belonged.

But then a sound louder than thunder erupted from the English side. Smoke, fire, and metal rained down on the French army. Soldiers fell to the ground wounded or killed by flying pieces of metal. Archers crumpled and horses bolted. The phalanx of the mighty French army scattered and fell into chaos.

What mysterious weapon did the English possess? Had they made a deal with the devil to pelt them with fire and brimstone? Had they harnessed the thunder of storms?

Their secret weapon was a new experiment for the Europeans. It was a cannon, and in 1346, Edward III was one of the first Europeans to use this invention in actual battle. People were used to seeing cannons mounted and defending the walls of castles or the fortifications around a town. But a cannon in the battlefield? It was unheard of. It was an experiment that was very successful for the English and King Edward III.

But then a sound louder than thunder erupted from the English side. Smoke, fire, and metal rained down on the French army.

The cannon was first developed in China. The Chinese who invented gunpowder also built metal tubes and filled them with shrapnel. The shrapnel might be anything from rocks or broken pottery to scraps of metal. When it was packed in the tube with gunpowder and lit on fire, the shrapnel flew through the air with deadly force, killing anything in its path.

The gunners or artillerymen who shot the cannons were considered to be elite troops. Shooting off a cannon was not just a matter of pouring a bunch of gunpowder into a barrel and setting it on fire. It required expert knowledge of gunpowder and chemistry of the day. If there was too much powder, the cannon itself could explode, killing the soldiers operating it. If the powder became damp, it wouldn't fire, and that could ruin battle plans.

Over time, inventors developed cannons in a great variety of lengths and diameters. They also

discovered that if they made the gunpowder coarser, it allowed air pockets to form around the grains of powder. This let the fire travel evenly and was much more efficient.

As more and more armies used the cannons, the walls around castles began to change. Cannon artillery could knock down almost any wall and allow the enemy to flood in and capture the castle. Builders had to create new ways to defend their castles and towns. They built thicker walls with angles and greater slopes.

The cannon and gunpowder totally changed how war was fought. The days of archers and knights were over. Cannons and eventually guns replaced the long bow and the sword. Castles disappeared and star-shaped forts became the defenses. It was an explosive experiment that changed the course of history.

SOBRERO'S SECRET

Model of nitroglycerine

Ascanio Sobrero was keeping a secret from the world. He had invented something so powerful, so dangerous, that he was afraid it could kill hundreds or even thousands of people. Sobrero feared his discovery could change the world forever.

In 1846, Sobrero was a professor at the University of Turin, Italy, and he was experimenting with nitric and sulfuric acids. One day, he tried mixing the acids with glycerol. Glycerol is a simple sugar alcohol that is used as a sweetener in drinks. It has an oily base and is used as a preservative to keep foods from drying out.

But when Sobrero mixed glycerol with nitric acid and heated it in a test tube, it caused a huge explosion. Broken glass flew through the air. Sobrero's face and hands were cut so badly that he had scars for the rest of his life.

Puzzled by the strange reaction, Sobrero studied the new compound. It was oily like the glycerin, but it was strangely volatile. A

He had invented something so powerful, so dangerous, that he was afraid it could kill hundreds or even thousands of people.

small amount heated in a test tube could cause a huge explosion. If it was frozen and then cooled, it could explode. If it was dropped, it could explode. But it didn't explode *every* time it was dropped, so it was unpredictable. There didn't seem to be any way to use the compound safely. It frightened Sobrero.

The compound he had just made was nitro-glycerine—an explosive many times more powerful than gunpowder. Just a tiny amount of the mixture

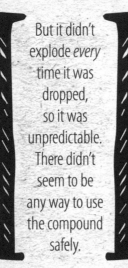

But it didn't explode *every* time it was dropped, so it was unpredictable. There didn't seem to be any way to use the compound safely.

caused huge explosions, and it was terribly unstable. But it was powerful. A few ounces of nitroglycerine could blow apart boulders and break parts of mountains. It would be so helpful to the engineers building the railroads.

But Sobrero also knew that it could be used as a tool of war. He was afraid of the horrible weapons that could be built to hurt soldiers and civilians. Because of this, he thought he should hide his discovery and not report his findings.

He hid his notes for a year, but then he realized that other chemists might experiment with the same chemicals. They might make the same discovery and be blown to pieces. He had to warn them.

Sobrero published a report about nitroglycerine and wrote numerous articles warning about the dangers of the chemical. He believed there was no safe means of handling the compound and that it should never be used as an explosive.

He often gave a demonstration to students who visited his lab to show how dangerous the compound was. He would rub a drop of nitroglycerine on an anvil and then strike the anvil with a hammer. The explosive sound was so loud that it made the students cover their ears. Sobrero asked them to imagine what might happen with more of the compound.

Ascanio Sobrero

To Sobrero's horror, some of the student did much more than imagine. They realized that there was money to be made if they could figure out how to control such a powerful explosive. Engineers,

builders, and international governments would be willing to pay great sums of money for such a powerful tool.

Many people experimented and many people died, and all of it dismayed Sobrero. He said, "When I think of all the victims killed during nitroglycerine explosions, and the terrible havoc that has been wreaked, which in all probability will continue to occur in the future, I am almost ashamed to admit to be its discoverer."

He would rub a drop of nitroglycerine on an anvil and then strike the anvil with a hammer. The explosive sound was so loud that it made the students cover their ears.

BIRTH OF DYNAMITE

Alfred Nobel was interested in anything that went BOOM! Of course he was: During the 1850s, his father owned a factory in St. Petersburg that produced explosives for the Russian government. Alfred grew up learning about underwater mines, cannonballs, and mortars. He knew how to mix gunpowder and set a fuse. Explosions were his business.

But when the Crimean War ended, the Russian tsar didn't need mines and bombs, and the Nobel

> Alfred grew up learning about underwater mines, cannonballs, and mortars. He knew how to mix gunpowder and set a fuse.

family factory went out of business. Alfred was determined to find a new way to use the family expertise. He had spent time studying chemistry abroad and had visited the Italian laboratory of Ascanio Sobrero. Nobel was one of the students who had seen Sobrero demonstrate the power of nitroglycerine. But the demonstration had not scared Alfred Nobel: It just made him determined to figure out a way to make nitroglycerine into a useable tool.

Nobel knew he was the right person for the job. He had expertise in explosives and formal training in chemistry. He was also careful and meticulous in his research. He did not want to risk hurting himself or any of the people who worked with him, so he tried to be cautious in his experiments.

Nobel learned that nitroglycerine was indeed a strange substance. Sometimes it would explode if it was simply dropped on the ground. But not all of the time. Nobel practiced throwing tubes of nitroglycerine in a ditch, and very few of the tubes exploded. He found that when the nitroglycerine was heated up, it would explode. But it didn't explode when it was touched with a flame. Then, it simply burned away.

This gave him an idea for how to set off a nitro-glycerine explosion while keeping a safe distance away. He put the nitroglycerine in a sealed metal tube. Suspended inside the tube was a sealed metal cap that contained gunpowder and a fuse. When the rope-like fuse was lit, it ignited the gunpowder. The detonation of the gunpowder set off the nitro-glycerine explosion.

Nobel spent weeks blowing up metal tubes until he was sure he had perfected his blasting cap. Now he knew he had solved a big part of the problem. He had a reliable way to make nitroglycerine explode.

In 1863, he filed with the Swedish patent office for an invention called the Nobel patent det-onator. Then Nobel went on the road to demonstrate his invention. He

Alfred Nobel

used his detonator to blast through rock in mines and railroad camps. The engineers and investors were impressed. So were the engineers who were building the Suez Canal in Egypt. A tool like this would greatly speed up construction.

Nobel was thrilled. His dreams of building back up the family business were coming true. He had investors willing to put up money for increased production. He hired a handyman and a chemist to help his brother in the Swedish laboratory. Excited by the prospect of a new business, they launched into production. But then tragedy struck.

One afternoon while Nobel was away from the lab, something went wrong. A blast shook the city of Stockholm. The Nobel laboratory was blown apart, and the explosion shook windows in buildings for blocks around. Alfred Nobel's younger brother and four other people were killed. The family was devastated. They didn't understand what had happened. Had one of the lab workers heated the nitroglycerine when they weren't supposed to? Had one of the caps gone off?

The citizens of Stockholm were furious. How could Nobel experiment with such a dangerous compound within the city limits? Officials demanded that he move the laboratory far away from the city.

Despite his brother's death, and the anger of the citizens of Stockholm, Nobel was determined to continue his experiments. He believed that his work with nitroglycerine could improve construction and provide safer ways to mine minerals. In the long run,

Excited by the prospect of a new business, they launched into production. But then tragedy struck.

he felt it could save lives and make the world a better place. His financial backer still believed that the Nobel detonator was a good idea and provided money for the project. Nobel built a new production plant out in the countryside of Sweden and went to work.

The more he experimented, the more he learned. But it didn't all go smoothly—there were more accidents. The nitroglycerine was still hard to handle, and it was corrosive to metal. If left in the metal tubes for too long, the nitroglycerine would break down the metal and leak out. Then, it caused unexpected explosions and terrible disasters. When more than 60 people were killed in three separate accidental nitroglycerine explosions in California, that state banned nitroglycerine as a blasting substance. The transcontinental railroad builders were only allowed to use gunpowder for their construction.

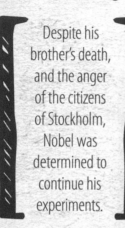

Despite his brother's death, and the anger of the citizens of Stockholm, Nobel was determined to continue his experiments.

Nobel was horrified by the accidental deaths and knew that he had to find a way to make nitroglycerine more stable. He experimented by mixing nitroglycerine with inert or very stable substances like sawdust and clay. Finally, he found a mixture that worked. He mixed nitroglycerine with kieselguhr, or diatomaceous earth. This is a sedimentary rock that easily crumbles into a fine white powder. When mixed with the nitroglycerine, it turned into a paste that could be kneaded and shaped into rods.

It didn't explode when it was dropped or thrown. It was safe to transport and store. At long last, Alfred had found the solution.

He decided to name his new invention after the Greek word for power: *dunamis*. In 1867, he received a patent for the invention of dynamite. It was the most powerful explosive the planet had ever seen, and it changed the world forever.

Recreation of Alfred Nobel's 1895 laboratory in the Nobel museum

ALFRED'S REVENGE

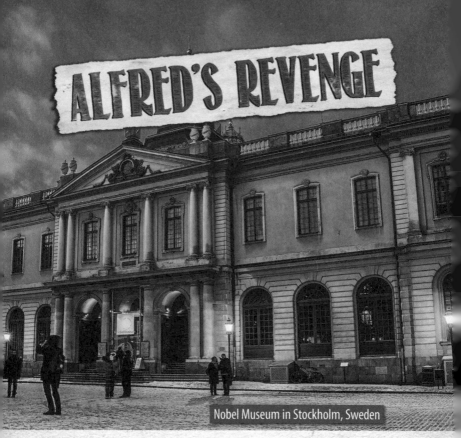

Nobel Museum in Stockholm, Sweden

It was a spring morning in Paris, and millionaire inventor Alfred Nobel had just sat down with the morning newspaper. When he opened the newspaper, he got the surprise of his life—or, rather, death. The paper declared that the inventor Alfred Nobel had died.

Nobel didn't have to pinch himself to know he wasn't dead. He knew the newspaper had made a terrible mistake. It was his brother Ludwig who had died. When Nobel read his own obituary, he was horrified to find out what people thought about him.

The headline read, "The Merchant of Death Is Dead." It went on to say, "Dr. Alfred Nobel, who became rich by finding ways to kill more people faster than ever before died yesterday . . . "

Nobel was horrified to read what the public thought of him. He believed his inventions could be used to better the world, and yet he was being depicted as a man who loved war and killing. He had to do something so that he would not be remembered as a person of war but a man of peace. He consulted with close friends and his lawyer to come up with a plan.

When Nobel died 7 years later, the world was amazed: He gave almost all of his vast fortune to set up a foundation that would award annual prizes to people who had made great contributions to humanity. The Nobel Prize was to be awarded for outstanding work in literature, science, and for promoting peace.

The first prizes were awarded in 1901, and since

that time there have been more than 500 prizes awarded for work in physics, chemistry, medicine, literature, peace, and economic studies. It is considered one of the most prestigious awards in the world.

Today the Nobel name is synonymous with the Nobel Prize. Nobel's legacy is one of encouraging the use of science for the peace and betterment of society.

NOBEL BY THE NUMBERS

Between 1901 and 2016, the Nobel Prizes and the Prize in Economic Sciences were awarded 579 times to 911 people and organizations, according to NobelPrize.org.

However, these numbers don't tell quite the full story—because a person or group can receive the prize more than once and because multiple people can be honored for the same prize (like a team of scientists working together), there's actually been a total of 881 individuals and 23 organizations who have collected the 579 prizes.

ARSENIC, ANYONE?

It looks like a simple white powder. It doesn't have any strange odor and has only a slight metallic taste. What is it? Arsenic, and just a pea-size dose of the poison will kill a grown man.

For centuries, assassins used arsenic to kill their targets. It was so simple. Invite your enemy over to a party and put a little arsenic in the wine. He or she would go home complaining of an upset stom-

> For centuries, assassins used arsenic to kill their targets. It was so simple. Invite your enemy over to a party and put a little arsenic in the wine.

ach and just hours later would be writhing in pain and vomiting violently. By morning, he or she would be dead from arsenic poisoning. And nobody suspected a thing, because in the Middle Ages (700–1200 AD) lots of people got food poisoning. Lots of people died from influenza or other stomach ailments. It was just considered an unfortunate death. Nobody could prove anything different.

The Borgias, a wealthy Italian family from the 1450s, became experts at arsenic poisoning. They killed off their enemies and took over their estates. Arsenic was the undetectable poison. No one could prove that the person had died from poisoning, so the killers always got away with murder.

In France, arsenic became known as inheritance powder, because it was given to elderly relatives to hurry up their death so the younger person could inherit the wealth. There was no known cure for arsenic poisoning, so eating or drinking it was almost always a death sentence.

But in 1833, a 22-year-old chemist named Robert Bunsen started experimenting to find a cure for the toxic drug. It was dangerous work. Just breathing the fumes of arsenic could possibly kill him. And some arsenic compounds can be so explosive that they will explode in dry air.

Bunsen invented a mask that covered his face and had a breathing tube that reached all the way outside his laboratory. The tube brought fresh air directly to his lungs so that he wouldn't pass out from fumes or inhale enough arsenic to kill him.

It took weeks of experimentation, but Bunsen finally came up with a solution. He learned that if he added iron oxide hydrate to a solution of arsenic, the molecules of the arsenic would bind to the iron and form the harmless compound of ferrous arsenate. It was the first hope for victims of arsenic poisoning.

The antidote would only work if the arsenic was still in the stomach and had not gone into the bloodstream, but it was a remedy that could save lives. And strangely, one life it saved was Robert Bunsen's.

Bunsen was a young and curious scientist who researched how to make batteries cheaper and learned how to analyze chemicals by the color of their flame. He perfected the Bunsen burner, which is still used in laboratories today. He was also curious about volcanoes and geysers and made a trip to Iceland so he could see just how geysers exploded.

But in 1843, Bunsen was back in his laboratory working with an arsenic compound called cacodyl cyanide when the chemical exploded. The blast shattered his facemask and permanently blinded Bunsen in his right eye. Noxious fumes of arsenic poured into his lungs. Bunsen was dying from arsenic poisoning.

Immediately, doctors administered the arsenic antidote that Bunsen himself had invented. It worked, and Bunsen regained his health. He went on to live to be an old man of 88 and spent his last years researching geology, not arsenic.

But in 1843, Bunsen was back in his laboratory working with an arsenic compound called cacodyl cyanide when the chemical exploded.

It was chemist James Marsh who figured out a way to detect arsenic in a person's body. In 1833, he developed the Marsh test—the first use of forensic toxicology in the world. When Charles Lafarge, a wealthy French foundry owner, died, his wife Marie was accused of feeding him arsenic. The Marsh test was used on the body and showed that arsenic was indeed present in his system. Marie Lafarge was convicted of killing her husband and spent the rest of her life in a French prison.

With Bunsen's antidote and Marsh's test, arsenic became much less popular as a killing agent. It is still used to kill rodents and as a poison, but anyone who tries to use it for murder will almost surely be caught.

FAMOUS
ARSENIC DEATHS

Arsenic used to be undetectable, but modern science can now detect arsenic poison from pieces of hair—even hair that is hundreds of years old. To prove whether some famous people were killed by arsenic, historians have dug up their bodies and had the hair tested. They found that several famous people were killed by the poison, but they still don't know if it was by accident or if it was murder.

Britain's King George III was rumored to be crazy, but historians thought his symptoms sounded like arsenic poisoning. They were right. Samples of his hair show unusually high levels of arsenic. But it could have been from the medicine doctors were using to treat him. It had arsenic, too.

Famous Emperor Napoleon Bonaparte died while he was exiled and imprisoned. His hair shows 13 times the normal levels of arsenic. But was it murder or was it from the arsenic in the environment? Historians are still trying to solve the mystery.

DEVIL'S PORRIDGE

Workers from HM Factory Gretna mixing the explosive cordite paste.

The British had a terrible problem. World War I was raging around them. The Germans were shelling their soldiers, and the Brits couldn't fight back. They didn't have enough ammunition. Without shells to shoot at their enemy, the British forces lost a huge battle at Neuve Chappelle in March of 1915. It was a disaster that could not happen again. It was a disaster that needed to be prevented.

World War I was raging around them. The Germans were shelling their soldiers, and the Brits couldn't fight back.

The project tasked with solving this problem went by the secret code name Moorside. It was the largest munitions plant in the world. The British military quickly put up manufacturing buildings in the town of Gretna, Scotland. The complex was 9 miles long and 2 miles wide and housed thousands of munitions workers, most of whom were women. They became known as the Gretna Girls, and their job was extremely dangerous.

The women were charged with making cordite—a smokeless explosive that was used to detonate ammunition. The women kneaded together the explosive nitroglycerine with gun cotton. The mixture was so volatile that the tiniest spark could cause the whole building to explode. It was nicknamed the devil's porridge. The women were checked daily before they entered the factory to make sure they didn't accidentally forget to remove a hairpin or an earring that might cause a spark.

By 1917, there were more than 9,000 women working at the factory—together, they produced 800 tons of cordite every week. They supplied the British military with the explosives they needed, but several young women lost their own lives making cordite. Some were killed in factory explosions, and others died from toxic fumes and poisoning. If the girls were exposed to too much sulfur, their skin would turn yellow. Sometimes the noxious gasses would cause the women's gums to bleed and their teeth would fall out. It is estimated that 300 young women died mixing up the devil's porridge.

CALL KINLEY

Myron Kinley

In 1913, Myron Kinley was just 15 years old, but he was an old pro at handling explosives. He started working for his father a couple years earlier, driving the wagon that carried loads of nitroglycerine to the California oil fields. His father taught him how to pack the nitroglycerine gel into metal canisters called torpedoes. Then he helped his father launch them precisely into the well in order to break apart the rock and increase the flow of oil out of the ground. It took a steady hand and calm nerves. The wrong move could cost Myron his life.

One morning, Myron's father got a call that would change everything. A well had blown its top and was shooting flames hundreds of feet into the air. The heat was so strong that men had to use metal shields to get close to the fire. The company was losing thousands of gallons of valuable oil, and the soot from the burning fuel was polluting the air. Water didn't dampen the inferno. Did Mr. Kinley have any ideas?

Myron went with his father to the site. He felt the heat waves rolling off the gigantic blaze. His father and his partner weren't sure what to do. They had never faced a fire like this. They knew from their work with explosives that a shockwave might be the way to push the burning and oxygen away from

> It took a steady hand and calm nerves. The wrong move could cost Myron his life.

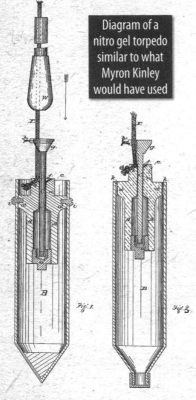

Diagram of a nitro gel torpedo similar to what Myron Kinley would have used

the well. It would be like blowing out a candle. But they would have to be careful, for as soon as the flame went out, the oxygen and other gasses would build back up. One spark could start another inferno.

Myron helped the men pack the 5-foot aluminum canisters with nitro gel, and then the team carefully lowered the torpedoes into the well. They were far away from it when the torpedoes exploded. Amazingly the fire went out. The force of the explosion blew the oxygen away from the fuel source and snuffed out the fire. Boiler trucks were then called to water down the well so it could be recapped. From that day on when a well was on fire, the oil field owners would say, "Call Kinley."

Myron took some time away from the family torpedo business to serve in World War I. He was assigned the duty of artilleryman. There probably weren't many soldiers more experienced with explosives than Myron.

When he returned, Myron teamed up with his younger brother, Floyd. Together they formed the M. M. Kinley Company and moved their headquarters to Houston, TX. Their specialty was fighting oil well fires. And there were lots of them to fight: In the 1920s and 1930s, oil was a new commodity. Scientists and engineers were just learning how to safely handle drilling. Both oil and gas wells had a nasty habit of blowing up.

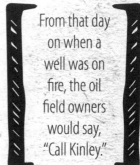

From that day on when a well was on fire, the oil field owners would say, "Call Kinley."

It was up to Myron to figure out new tools to help with the job and new ways to put out the fires. And he got very good at it. In his career, he helped blow up and extinguish more than 600 oil and gas fires. He developed a special trolley system that could be used to clear debris from the oil well and help place the explosives. He received patents for numerous tools that are still used in fighting fires.

Although Myron lost his brother and business partner, Floyd, in a well fire in 1936, he kept on fighting fires and inventing new and better way to use explosives to stop the flames. He was wounded several times and spent weeks in the hospital recovering from burns and broken bones. An injury to his leg left him with a limp for the rest of his life, but he felt that fighting fires was his calling. He kept working despite the loss of friends and the threat to his own health. He died in 1978 at the age of 80. The petroleum industry considers him the father of oil well firefighters and an innovator in the use of explosives.

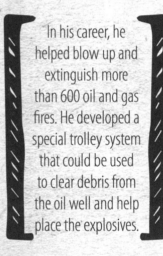

In his career, he helped blow up and extinguish more than 600 oil and gas fires. He developed a special trolley system that could be used to clear debris from the oil well and help place the explosives.

Science Lab

GROW YOUR OWN CRYSTALS

n the Middle Ages, farmers and workers had to grow their own saltpeter crystals. You can grow crystals, too, but these won't be used to make gunpowder. They just look cool.

47

MATERIALS

- » Large container of alum (alum is found in the spices section of the grocery store and is used in making pickles)
- » Plastic Easter eggs
- » Paintbrush
- » 2 plastic or glass cups
- » 1 cup very hot water
- » 2–3 cup size bowl
- » Spoon
- » Paper towels

Squirt a little glue into each "egg shell" and spread it evenly over the inside of the shell. Then sprinkle a layer of alum crystals all over the glue. Let this dry overnight.

Heat one cup of hot water in the microwave until it is boiling (you will need an adult to help with this part).

Add alum to the hot water until the mixture is saturated (that means to add alum until no more will melt in the hot water). It takes about 6 tablespoons per cup of hot water. (If you have grainy alum in the bottom of your water, you have added too much.)

Add your favorite color of food coloring or egg dye and let it dissolve.

Place each eggshell in its own plastic glass or cup with the open side up. Pour the alum solution over the egg until it is completely covered. Then set it aside for at least 15 hours.

Check it later to see how the crystals have grown.

Science Lab

EXPLODING BAGGIES

The Chinese learned that mixing chemicals can cause an explosion. You can make your own chemical explosion with this experiment. (Don't worry! It will be much less dangerous than gunpowder!)

MATERIALS

» Sandwich bag with ziplock closure

» Tissue

» 1/4 cup water

» 1/2 cup vinegar

» 3 tablespoons baking soda

Do this experiment outside. It can get messy!

Open your plastic bag and add water and vinegar. Seal it shut.

Then unfold the tissue and add the baking soda to the center of the tissue. Fold it up into a little square so that none of the baking soda falls out.

Open the corner of your baggie and drop the tissue of baking soda inside. Quickly reseal the baggie. Then stand back and watch!

The baking soda will make a chemical reaction with the vinegar to create the gas carbon dioxide. This will cause the bag to inflate and explode.

Science Lab

PAINT BOMBS

ou can make art with explosions! All you need are a few paint bombs, and you can create a masterpiece.

MATERIALS

- » Several colors of powdered tempera paint (available at all craft and art stores)
- » Sandwich bags with ziplock closure
- » Vinegar
- » Poster board
- » Outdoor area
- » Measuring cups
- » Measuring spoons

This activity is very messy, so it has to be done outside. Ask an adult to help you find a good place for this experiment.

Lay the poster board on the ground. You will need to make one paint bomb and then release it onto the poster board before you make the next paint bomb.

Take a baggie and pour in 1/3 cup of vinegar. Add two tablespoons of powdered tempera paint. Seal the bag and lay it on the poster board. Watch as the paint and vinegar react, filling the baggie with gas. Let it explode and create an abstract painting. Then fill another baggie with a different color of tempera paint and vinegar. Let it explode. Do this as many times with as many colors as you like. When you have finished, let the poster board dry, then show your paint bomb masterpiece to the world!

HINDENBURG
DISASTER

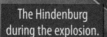

The Hindenburg during the explosion.

In 1936, the Hindenburg was the height of luxury. It was one of two gas-filled dirigibles that carried passengers across the Atlantic Ocean at the amazing speed of 84 miles per hour.

The Hindenburg provided its passengers with every comfort they could imagine. They had a carpeted dining room with plush chairs and white tablecloths. The passengers had sleeping rooms where they could snooze the night away. If they didn't want to sleep, there was also a bar or a smoking room. It was a pleasant way to spend 2 days flying over the ocean, and it was much faster than the 5-day crossing by ship.

The Hindenburg and its sister ship, the Graf Zeppelin, were the result of decades of experimenting with gas-filled airships. They had been implemented successfully during World War I for observation and some bombing missions, but in the 1930s, the zeppelins were used for the peaceful purposes of air travel and delivery of mail. Of course, it was air travel for the very rich. Today, a ticket on the Hindenburg would cost the equivalent of $8,000.

The Hindenburg was designed to be a helium ship. Helium and hydrogen are both gasses that are lighter than air, and both were used to fill the balloon-like ships to make them

The Hindenburg provided its passengers with every comfort they could imagine. They had a carpeted dining room with plush chairs and white tablecloths.

float. Hydrogen had been used in many airships because it was lighter than helium, and therefore the ships could be smaller. But there had been some accidents with hydrogen ships that had resulted in fires. Hydrogen is much more flammable than helium. The makers of the Hindenburg decided to build a helium ship and knew it had to be larger than a hydrogen ship in order to get enough lift to carry the same payload.

When the Hindenburg was finished, it was 803 feet long with a diameter of 135 feet. It was three times longer than a Boeing 747. It was one of the largest ships that ever flew.

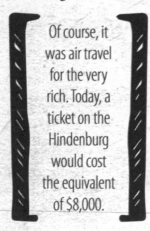

Of course, it was air travel for the very rich. Today, a ticket on the Hindenburg would cost the equivalent of $8,000.

But what the Germans had not counted on was the short supply of helium. The United States controlled most of the helium supply in the world, and after fighting the Germans in World War I, the Americans were not willing to sell the German company any of their helium. The Hindenburg would have to be filled with hydrogen after all.

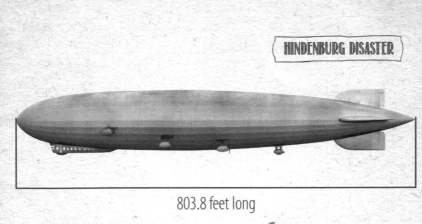

803.8 feet long

231.8 feet long

During 1936, the Hindenburg crossed the Atlantic 34 times, transporting more than 3,500 passengers and more than 66,000 pounds of mail and cargo. The press was awestruck with the amazing ship and covered its flights on radio and in the newspapers. Unlike the airplanes of the day, the dirigibles did not have to stop to refuel, so their flights were actually more efficient. It appeared that the Germans had invented the best form of air travel.

In 1937, the Hindenburg took passengers back and forth from Germany to Brazil. It made six successful flights before it was scheduled for its first North American flight of the season. The ship left Germany on May 3, 1937 with 36 paying passengers and a large crew of 61 that included both officers and junior crew members in training.

Just 3 days later, the ship floated over the city of Boston on its way to New York City. It flew past the New York skyscrapers at 3 p.m. and headed south to land at the Naval Air Station at Lakehurst, NJ. Stormy weather caused the captain to delay landing until 7 p.m. When the giant ship sailed over the airfield, the ship slowed down and the mooring lines were dropped so the ship could be anchored. The ship was at an altitude of 295 feet.

A crowd had gathered on the ground to watch the Hindenburg land. As they looked up, they saw flames shoot from the tail of the ship. In seconds, the entire rear of the plane was on fire. The volatile hydrogen gas lit up like a giant blow torch and the tail fell to the ground. The fire spread to the rest of the ship in less than a minute. Passengers and crew knew their only hope of survival was to jump from the windows of the promenade deck.

Reporters who had been there to cover the landing of the famous German ship filmed the trag-

See the Hindenburg
You can view the actual newsreel that was shown in movie theatres in 1937 at https://www.youtube.com/watch?v=rWe01q0gHJE

edy as it happened. Eyewitnesses watched as people jumped from the burning inferno. Some made it to safety, and others died in the attempt. Amazingly, 62 people survived the crash and fire while 35 passengers and crew members died.

That fiery crash marked the end of the dirigible as a means of commercial air transportation. When the world witnessed the explosion on newsreel film, they became terrified of flying in a dirigible. The great zeppelin experiment was over.

DEADLIEST AIRSHIPS

Because the Hindenburg explosion was caught on film, it remains the most famous airship disaster, but it wasn't the deadliest. The *USS Akron*, a Navy airship, crashed in a storm off the coast of New Jersey in 1933, killing 73 men. There were only three survivors. The British military also had an airship crash that was more deadly than the Hindenburg—the airship R101 crashed in 1930 and killed 48 people.

THE EXPLODING SCHOOL

New London school explosion debris.

You'd never expect your school to explode, but that's exactly what happened to the students and teachers of New London, TX.

It was a warm March day in 1937. The younger students had been dismissed at 2:30 p.m., but grades 5–11 had a longer school day. Students were busy working in shop class, studying in the library, and experimenting in the science lab, while a parent meeting was going on in the gymnasium.

The New London School was one of the wealthiest in Texas because of the natural gas that had been discovered in the area. The families were proud of their large campus and very modern science labs.

But what nobody knew was that the school board had been experimenting with how to heat the school building. When it was first built, the school district paid nearly $300 a month to pipe in gas from the nearby gas fields. But then some of the board members decided that a great way to save money was to tap into a pipeline of residual gas. This was a common practice for many homes and offices

Students were busy working in shop class, studying in the library, and working in the science lab, while a parent meeting was going on in the gymnasium.

in the community. The residual gas was a waste product of the gas companies and was being burned off. It was free to the school and saved the district $300 a month.

But the connection to the residual gas line began to leak, and because natural gas is odorless and colorless, no one knew that a huge amount of gas was

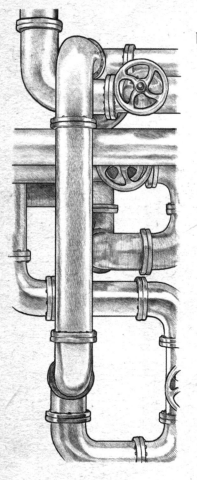

building up underneath the school—just waiting for a spark to set it off.

At 3:05 that afternoon, the shop teacher flipped a switch to turn on a sanding machine, and immediately the entire school building lifted in the air, then smashed back to the ground. The walls collapsed and the roof crashed in, burying students and teachers in a mass of brick and steel. The blast was so powerful it was heard 4 miles away.

Within minutes, people from the area had congregated at the school. They were met with a ghastly site. Bodies of children and teachers were scattered over the schoolyard, and the school itself was a pile of rubble.

Roughnecks from the East Texas oilfield came immediately, bringing heavy equipment to dig out survivors. The governor sent the Texas Rangers in to help with the rescue, and hundreds of other volunteers, from Boy Scouts to the Red Cross, came and dug through the crumbled bricks and crushed cement to pull out anyone who had survived.

In just 17 hours, the volunteers had found all the victims and removed all the debris. The injured were taken to the hospital, and the dead were put in makeshift mortuaries where their families could identify the bodies. Out of the 500 students and 40 teachers in the school, 298 died. More than 120 were seriously injured, and only about 130 people escaped with minor injuries.

In the weeks after the explosion, it was discovered that the school board had tapped into the residual line, but a judge ruled that there was no way that the school board could have known that there was a gas leak that endangered the students.

Because of this, the state of Texas passed an odorization law that required gas companies to put malodorants (chemicals that smell bad) into all the gas used by homes and businesses. This way people would know when there was a gas leak because they would be able to smell it. Eventually this became the standard for gas companies around the world, and that is why the gas in homes today has a slight odor. It is to prevent another school explosion like the one in New London.

Out of the 500 students and 40 teachers in the school, 298 died. More than 120 were seriously injured, and only about 130 people escaped with minor injuries.

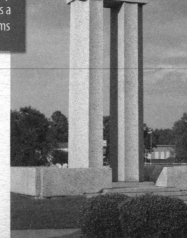

The New London Cenotaph was erected in 1939 as a memorial to the victims of the explosion

TICKLING THE DRAGON'S TAIL

A recreation of the criticality experiment that Slotin conducted.

It was called "tickling the dragon's tail"—an experiment so dangerous that it could be as deadly as dragon fire. And Louis Slotin was the world expert on tickling that dragon. But in 1946, Slotin made a horrible mistake that cost him his life.

After working on the top secret Manhattan Project to build the first atomic bomb, Slotin was retiring from Los Alamos and headed to a teaching position. He had spent years experimenting with the most dangerous chemicals in the world. During WWII, he worked with scientist Enrico Fermi to create the first nuclear chain reaction.

He understood the strange properties of pluto-nium and beryllium, and how they could be com-bined to trigger an atomic nuclear reaction. (This is similar to the way a blasting cap is used to set off otherwise stable dynamite.) At the end of WWII, Slotin was one of the few men in the world who knew how to build an atomic bomb by hand.

And on May 21, 1946, he was teaching coworker Alvin Graves how to tickle that dragon's tail. A very precisely shaped and weighed mass of plutonium was called the *core*, and two half-shells of beryllium, fashioned a certain way, were called the *tamper*. As long as the core rested in only the bottom half of the tamper, the core was not too dangerous. But as the top half of the tam-per was lowered down on top, closing in the core, the core would emit rap-idly increasing amounts of dangerous X-ray radia-tion. The core would then

> It was called "tickling the dragon's tail"—an experiment so dangerous that it could be as deadly as dragon fire.

go "super-critical." For lab experiments, scientists wanted to get *close* to super-critical but keep the top half of the tamper from getting *too* close. Instruments (called *Geiger counters*) nearby would tell them just how close they had gotten.

Amazingly, the tool that Slotin always used to keep the tamper halves apart was a simple screwdriver. He had done this job many times before, and had never had a problem, but on that fateful day in May, his screwdriver slipped. The tamper half-shells clinked together, and a blue flash filled the room. Heat from the reaction washed over the six scientists and a security guard present.

Slotin knew immediately what had happened, and threw his body over the experiment to shield his friends from the radiation. Then he batted away the top half of the shell to stop the reaction from going critical. As the shell clinked to the floor, a bitter taste came into Slotin's mouth. Everyone had been exposed to huge doses of radiation. An ambulance was called, and the men were rushed to the hospital.

[Slotin knew immediately what had happened, and threw his body over the experiment to shield his friends from the radiation.]

To help the doctors figure out how much radiation each person had received, Slotin drew a sketch of where each person was standing in the room. Slotin threw up several times from the radiation and his left hand was numb, but other than that he seemed to be normal. When he was examined at the Los Alamos hospital, it was discovered that he had taken 2,100 rem of neutrons, gamma rays, and X-rays (500 rem is considered a fatal dose). Slotin's left hand took on a waxy blue color and developed large blisters. Doctors had to keep it packed in ice to limit the pain. Doctors said that Slotin had radiation burns over his whole body, both inside and out. One doctor compared it to a three-dimensional sunburn.

Slotin's parents were flown in from Canada and were able to tell their son goodbye. Slotin died 9 days after the accident. The other seven scientists were able to be treated for radiation poisoning and did not die immediately. Years later, three of the scientists did develop health complications that contributed to their death. But Slotin died knowing that he had saved his friends from immediate death.

After that accident, the laboratory at Los Alamos halted all experiments involving setting up nuclear explosions by hand. Future experiments used remote controls and safety shields and moved scientists farther away from radiation.

When Slotin died, his body still had so much radiation that he had to be buried in a casket with a lead liner so that his body would not give off radiation poisoning in the cemetery.

Louis Slotin with the Gadget bomb

BROKEN ARROWS

The United States military code name for an accident involving a nuclear weapon is *Broken Arrow*. The accident may involve an unexpected detonation like the one caused by

A drawing that shows where Slotin's team would have been positioned during the accident

Louis Slotin, or it could be an accidental launch or firing of a nuclear weapon. Since 1950, there have been 32 Broken Arrows in the world.

The last one recorded happened in August of 2000, when a CIS (Commonwealth of Independent States) submarine sank after a massive explosion. It is believed that a torpedo failure caused the explosion that killed 118 members of the sub crew.

THE ATOMIC BOMB

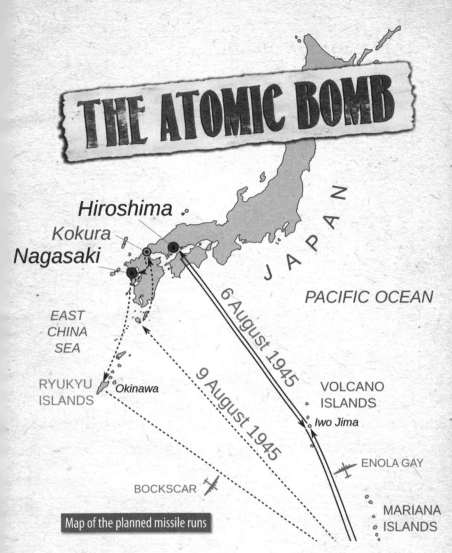

Map of the planned missile runs

It was early morning August 6, 1945, and Luis Alvarez was strapped into the seat of a B-29 Superfortress speeding to the islands of Japan. He was one of the team of scientists assigned to observe the world's biggest man-made explosion: the dropping of the atomic bomb on Hiroshima.

Alvarez had done the critical work of inventing the detonator for the 9,000-pound uranium bomb, nicknamed Little Boy. He had also created a set of calibrated microphone transmitters designed to measure the strength of the blast from the explosion. The device was to be parachuted out of the plane and would send readings back for scientists to study.

Alvarez and the crew tried to remain calm on their mission. They knew it was a critical move by the Allies. World War II had been raging for nearly 6 years. In May, Hitler's army had finally surrendered, but the Japanese emperor vowed to fight on. The Allies were weary of war. They had lost millions of soldiers and civilians and knew that an invasion of Japan would cost more lives.

On July 26, the United States joined with Great Britain and China to issue The Potsdam Declaration that threatened Japan with "prompt and utter destruction" if they did not immediately surrender. When the Japanese did not respond, President Harry Truman approved the decision to drop the

Little Boy, atomic bomb

atomic bomb. On August 6, Alvarez and the rest of the crews were in three B-29s headed for Japan.

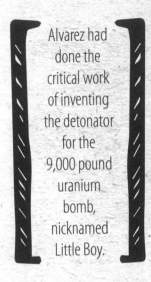

Alvarez had done the critical work of inventing the detonator for the 9,000 pound uranium bomb, nicknamed Little Boy.

The lead plane was the *Enola Gay*, named after the pilot's mother. Alvarez and the other scientists followed in a plane named *The Great Artiste*. A third plane called *Necessary Evil* served as the photography aircraft.

By late morning, the planes had reached the target site. Alvarez could see the main island through the puffs of white clouds. The Japanese could see the planes and fired on them. Flak exploded near the planes, but none were hit. The formation flew on with the lead plane, *Enola Gay*, moving ahead of the other two aircrafts.

Just after noon, the radio crackled, and Alvarez and the rest of the scientists put on their welder's goggles to protect their eyes from the brightness of the blast.

"There she goes," someone shouted, and Alvarez could see the body of Little Boy drop from the belly of *Enola Gay*. As the bomb sank into the clouds, the pilots turned the planes away in the opposite direction. They needed to get as far away as possible from the blast. Then the cabin of the plane was filled with a bright light that broke through the darkness of the welder's goggles. Alvarez knew it was the bomb releasing its energy. The plane filled with a bluish-green light.

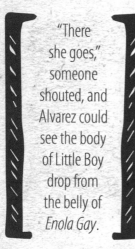

"There she goes," someone shouted, and Alvarez could see the body of Little Boy drop from the belly of *Enola Gay*.

Then suddenly a blast hit the plane, causing it to shake violently from nose to tail. It was followed by more blasts that sounded as loud as cannon fire. Alvarez and the other scientists watched as a giant ball of fire rose into the sky. Purple flames flew 10,000 feet into the air. Then a cloud of gas rolled into the sky, forming a gigantic mushroom. Alvarez's detonation device had worked, and he had witnessed the first use of an atomic weapon against an enemy.

It is estimated that the explosion killed 70,000–80,000 people in Hiroshima. Sadly, the Japanese emperor refused to surrender. The Japanese military leaders believed the Allies could only get one or maybe two more bombs ready to drop. They decided that their people would just have to endure the attacks. They believed that their war would still go forward.

On August 9, Alvarez was strapped back in his seat on the Flying Fortress. This time, the mission was to drop Fat Man, a 10,800-pound plutonium bomb. This bomb was destined for the city of Nagasaki. At 11 a.m., Alvarez's plane dropped his instruments attached to a parachute. A few minutes later, Fat Man exploded over Nagasaki.

Eventually, the Japanese Emperor agreed to surrender to the Allied forces. Some of the Emperor's military officers did not want to believe that the surrender was real, leading to a brief attempt at rebellion. But the Emperor formally announced the surrender in a radio broadcast on August 15, and it was accepted by the Allies.

Fat Man,
atomic bomb

This time, the mission was to drop Fat Man, a 10,800-pound plutonium bomb. This bomb was destined for the city of Nagasaki.

On September 2, 1945, Alvarez was one of the millions of relieved Allies who celebrated the official end of WWII with the surrender of Japan. He later said that although they had been horribly destructive, the bombs had done their job and ended the war.

After the war, Alvarez went on to experiment with particle accelerators and received a Nobel Peace Prize for his work in physics. He held numerous scientific patents and even invented a golf training device for President Dwight D. Eisenhower. He died in 1988 at the age of 77 from cancer.

Bombing of Hiroshima

RADIOACTIVE JAPAN?

Because both Little Boy and Fat Man were detonated in the air high above Japan, the radioactive fireball did not touch the ground. This dramatically reduced the amount of radiation that fell on Nagasaki and Hiroshima. Because of this, the background radiation on these two cities is now .87mSv/a— the same level as most of the world.

APOLLO 13 EXPLOSION

The space flight was going well. The Apollo 13 crew were 200,000 miles from Earth and were closing in on the moon. A few more hours, and they would begin orbit. This would be the third team of U.S. astronauts to walk on the moon. Americans were confident that this trip would be just as successful as the last two.

But on April 13, 1970, everything changed. Mission control got a low-pressure warning on a hydrogen tank. They radioed astronaut Jack Swigert and told him to do a routine "cryo stir" to make sure the super cold gas was not settling into layers. Swigert flipped the switch, and seconds later, there was a loud bang and the entire spacecraft shook. Alarm lights lit up, and oxygen pressure

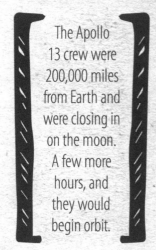

The Apollo 13 crew were 200,000 miles from Earth and were closing in on the moon. A few more hours, and they would begin orbit.

dropped. Power supplies plummeted. Something was terribly wrong.

Swigert radioed Mission Control and said, "Houston, we've had a problem." The space crew could look out the window and see gas venting out of the hatch.

An investigation would later show that a spark from exposed wire in the oxygen tank had caused a fire, exploding one oxygen tank and damaging another one inside the spacecraft. Mission Control immediately went into action, telling the astronauts to shut down all nonessential systems. Apollo 13 would not be landing on the moon. They would be lucky to return to Earth alive.

The astronauts shut down the command module completely to save energy so it could be used for re-entry to the Earth's atmosphere. They moved into the Lunar Landing Module and powered it up to use it like a life boat to stay alive until they could get back to Earth.

It was going to be a cold and difficult journey home. They had to use some of their limited fuel to do a controlled burn that would give the ship the right trajectory home. Then they had to survive temperatures near freezing and a shortage of food and water. Worse, the air scrubbers stopped working,

Apollo 13 space capsule

so the levels of breathable oxygen were decreasing. Mission Control experimented with the supplies they knew were on board the space capsule until they found a combination that worked. Then the astronauts had to follow mission control's instructions to rig up a modified air scrubber.

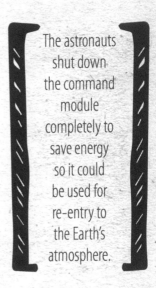

The astronauts shut down the command module completely to save energy so it could be used for re-entry to the Earth's atmosphere.

It was a long 4 days, with Americans glued to their television sets and radios waiting to see if the three astronauts would survive. On April 17, the Apollo 13 command module was powered back up, and the astronauts safely splashed down in the South Pacific.

The ultimate success of the mission was due to the ingenuity of the scientists and astronauts and their willingness to experiment until they found answers. It was an explosion that led to changes in how future spacecraft were designed and built. It was also one of the most dramatic stories in space exploration.

RUSSIAN SPACE EXPLORATIONS

The United States is not the only country to have its space experiments explode. The Russians have had several accidents in their rocket program. The worst was called the Nedelin Catastrophe. It happened in 1960 when the Russians were experimenting with long-range missiles called *intercontinental ballistic missiles* (ICBM).

One of these missiles, R-16 ICBM, was more than 95 feet long and weighed 141 tons. Fueled with an unstable compound called Devil's Venom, the rocket exploded on the launch pad. The explosion was so powerful that it vaporized the bodies of some of the engineers working on the site. In all, it killed 150 people and was one of the worst space explosions in history.

STARFISH PRIME

Artificial aurora lights the sky over the Pacific Ocean following the Starfish Prime space nuclear explosion.

They called it a *rainbow bomb party*, and everyone in Honolulu was invited to attend. You could pull out your lawn chair and watch from your backyard, or if you wanted to spend a few bucks, you could watch the explosion from a hotel rooftop while you enjoyed drinks and snacks. Sounds like a big fireworks celebration, but it was actually the launch of a 1.45 megaton atomic bomb project called *Starfish Prime*, and it literally shook the world.

You could pull out your lawn chair and watch from your backyard, or if you wanted to spend a few bucks, you could watch the explosion from a hotel rooftop while you enjoyed drinks and snacks.

Why would anyone think it was a good idea to launch a nuclear bomb 100 times larger than the atomic bombs that were dropped in WWII? Because in 1962, America was in the middle of a cold war with the Soviet Union, which had a few months earlier tested nuclear weapons in outer space. The United States government had to prove it had the same destructive capabilities as its enemy.

So on the night of July 9, 1962, the U.S. military launched a Thor missile from Johnston Island, about 900 miles south of Hawaii. The missile flew up to a peak height of 660 miles above the Earth, then arced back down. When it reached the pre-programmed height of 240 miles above Earth, the atomic bomb was detonated.

People attending the bomb parties definitely saw a light show. Artificial aurora borealis filled the

night sky
with bands
of green, purple,
red, and orange lights.
The explosion was so
powerful that people in
New Zealand reported seeing the lights.

Then the lights in Hawaii went out. The electric lights in homes, hotels, and businesses blinked off and stayed off. All electric power was gone. The blast from the bomb caused an electromagnetic pulse that knocked out both civilian and military electrical systems. It also damaged more than a third of the satellites in orbit around the Earth.

The United States military learned from its experiments. And the lessons caused the military to rethink its use of such devastating weapons. They realized how such explosions could be used to take out the electrical power to a major city or part of a foreign country. It started research into a new class of weapons called Non-Nuclear Electromagnetic Pulse weapons.

The Soviet Union and United States continued to test nuclear weapons until the end of the Cold

War. The last nuclear test done by the U.S. was in 1992, and it was the first country to sign the international Comprehensive Nuclear Test-Ban Treaty in 1996.

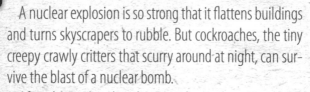

COCKROACH SURVIVORS

A nuclear explosion is so strong that it flattens buildings and turns skyscrapers to rubble. But cockroaches, the tiny creepy crawly critters that scurry around at night, can survive the blast of a nuclear bomb.

After the nuclear bombs were dropped on Hiroshima, stories spread that cockroaches were some of the only animals to survive a direct hit. To see if this could possibly be true, the television show *MythBusters* tested cockroaches by exposing them to the radioactive metal cobalt-60. A 10-minute exposure of 1,000 radon units will kill a human, but not a cockroach. Half of the cockroaches survived that amount of radiation. And some even survived 10,000 radon units. It took 100,000 radon units to kill all of the cockroaches in the test group. It may be true that cockroaches will inherit the Earth.

CHERNOBYL BLOWS

The Scandinavians were the first to know that something terrible had happened in the Soviet Union. On the morning of April 26, 1986, monitoring stations pinged and beeped. Scientists looked at the readings and were astonished. There was a radioactive cloud blowing into the country, and it had to come from the USSR. But there had been no word of any problem from Soviet officials. What was going on?

It was one of the worst nuclear accidents in history. In the very early hours of April 26, the nuclear power plant called Chernobyl had experienced a disastrous chain reaction at the core of reactor No. 4. A steam explosion erupted in a giant fireball that blew the roof off the reactor and released huge quantities of radioactive particles into the atmosphere.

The amount of radiation in the plant itself was measured at 20,000 roentgens per hour. A lethal dose of radiation is 500 roentgens over a 5-hour period. The workers inside the plant received a fatal dose of radiation in less than a minute. None of them wore protective gear, and those who were not killed in the immediate blast stayed to try to get the fire under control.

Firefighters arrived quickly to help put out the blaze. They did not know how much radiation they were getting as they tried to put out the fire with water hoses. They were able to get the fire out on the roof, but many of the firefighters also received fatal doses of radiation. The fire inside reactor No. 4 kept burning for 2 weeks. It was finally put out when helicopters dropped more than 5,000 tons of sand, lead, and clay on the reactor. Firefighters and nuclear plant workers were taken to the hospital for examination—28 of them died within 3 weeks from acute radiation poisoning.

A steam explosion erupted in a giant fireball that blew the roof off the reactor and released huge quantities of radioactive particles into the atmosphere.

The Soviet Union did not want to admit to what happened at Chernobyl. It was only when other countries in Europe began asking questions about the high radiation readings that the USSR recognized that its experiment had gone horribly wrong.

For a full day, the Soviets did not even tell the residents of the town closest to Chernobyl what had happened. Many residents knew that something was going on because they saw the smoke and blue glowing fire from the reactor that was 3 miles away. When Soviet officials finally told the people that there had been an explosion, the people believed that they were going to be taken on a bus to a decontamination site. The residents all believed they would be sent back in 3 days, so they just brought a few items with them. What they did not know was that the Soviet officials were declaring their town a nuclear disaster site, and they would never be able to return.

The area around the Chernobyl nuclear reactor has been declared an exclusion zone where no one

This is the first photograph ever taken of the accident, and the only photo that survives from the morning of the accident. Igor Kostin was a photographer from Kiev who became world famous for his images of the clean-up operation. The image is very noisy because the radiation was destroying the film in his camera. Of all the shots he took on that flight, this is the only one that wasn't ruined.

is allowed to live or even visit without special permission. The exclusion zone is nearly 1,000 square miles in size. That is almost as big as the state of Rhode Island.

The results of the failed Chernobyl experiment were felt worldwide. Nuclear energy had been very popular as a new energy source, but now people around the world were scared of radiation poisoning. They feared that the nuclear power plant near their town could explode and ruin thousands of miles of forest or crop land, so governments stopped the new construction of nuclear plants. Today, nuclear power is still a controversial topic.

NUKE STATS

In the 1950s, nuclear energy was advertised as clean, safe energy that could power our world without smog and air pollution. Scientists had demonstrated that splitting an atom could do more than just make powerful explosions: it could also be used to create electricity. A pellet of uranium the size of a pencil eraser could make as much electricity as 1,780 pounds of coal.

~continues on page 94~

NUKE STATS

~continued from page 93~

People were so excited about nuclear energy that they began thinking of themselves as living in the new "atomic age." Politicians were thrilled with this new form of energy and encouraged companies to build nuclear power plants. Some scientists believed that by the year 2000, the United States would get all of its electricity from hundreds of very efficient nuclear plants.

But as nuclear power plants were built around the world, people learned that there were some definite drawbacks to nuclear energy. The biggest problem was waste disposal. Using nuclear energy creates waste materials that are radioactive and can cause diseases like cancer. Too much radiation can poison and kill the human body. Nuclear waste must be stored in specially designed containers that will block the radiation from harming the environment.

Today there are 444 nuclear power plants operating in 30 countries around the world. France gets more than 75% of its energy from nuclear power. The United States has 99 nuclear plants that supply 20% of the total power in the country.

TSAR BOMBA

It was an experiment ordered by Soviet Union leader Nikita Khrushchev. And in 1961, no one living in the USSR wanted to say no to Khrushchev—not if they wanted to stay out of prison. So the scientists of the USSR scrambled to create Tsar Bomba, the largest nuclear bomb in the world.

Khrushchev wanted to show the world his military power by exploding a hydrogen bomb in the skies over the Arctic Circle. He set the test date for October, when the Congress of the Communist Party would be meeting, and told the scientists to get busy.

In an amazing 15 weeks, a team of four scientists was able to invent a hydrogen bomb that weighed 27 tons and was 27 feet long. The bomb was so big that they had to cut off a plane's bomb bay doors to get it loaded.

The experiment launched on October 30, when the plane dropped Tsar Bomba from a height of 6.5 miles above the Earth. The bomb was parachuted down to a height of 2.5 miles and then detonated. The flash of light was so brilliant it could be seen 500 miles away. It created a fireball 6 miles high and a mushroom cloud 40 miles high. The shock wave felt like an earthquake and shattered windows 500 miles away in Norway and

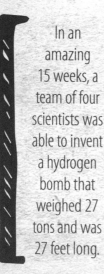

In an amazing 15 weeks, a team of four scientists was able to invent a hydrogen bomb that weighed 27 tons and was 27 feet long.

Finland. It could have given off deadly radiation, but the scientists used lead tampers that prevented 97% of nuclear fallout.

Khrushchev was thrilled with the results of his experiment. It was the largest bomb ever exploded, and he had shown the world what his military could do. It also helped bring about a worldwide partial ban on above-ground nuclear testing. That treaty was signed in 1963 to prevent another Tsar Bomba from being tested.

STRONGEST BOMBS IN THE WORLD

Over the years scientists have created some very powerful explosives. Some of them, like Tsar Bomba, were detonated; others, however, were created but never used in wars. Here are some of the most powerful bombs the world has ever seen.

GBU-43 MOAB

Nicknamed the Mother of all Bombs, this nonnuclear bomb was put into service by the U.S. military in 2003.

~continues on page 98~

STRONGEST BOMBS IN THE WORLD

~continued from page 97~

MOAB is 30 feet long and weighs 21,000 lbs. It is designed to burst 6 feet above the ground so that it will increase its destructive range. It has never been used in war.

W54 nuclear warhead

It may only be 15 1/2 inches long, but this little bomb could pack quite a wallop. Created in the 1950s, this small bomb could flatten the buildings in two city blocks. This type of warhead was deactivated without ever being used in a war.

FOAB

Called the Father of All Bombs, this Russian bomb was built in response to the U.S.'s MOAB. This bomb is four times more powerful than MOAB and explodes in midair. It causes a supersonic shockwave that vaporizes every-thing in its target range.

EXPLODING ELEMENTS

1	**Hydrogen**	H

Atomic mass: 1.008
Electron configuration: 1

92	**Uranium**	U

Atomic mass: 238.02
Electron configuration: 2, 8, 18, 32, 21, 9, 2

55	**Caesium**	Cs

Atomic mass: 132.90
Electron configuration: 2, 8, 18, 18, 8, 1

When people think of explosions, they usually imagine a scientist in the lab sloshing chemicals from one beaker to another. She mixes the wrong chemicals and—Kaboom!—it's an explosion. But in reality, scientists don't have to mix up any fancy chemical compound, because several explosive elements are naturally found in the Earth's crust.

Uranium (U) became famous because it was used to create the first nuclear bomb. Scientists had to manipulate the isotopes to make uranium explosive in today's environment. But when the Earth was young and the planet had more volcanoes and hot lava flowing, uranium exploded naturally. Geologists have found evidence of spontaneously occurring nuclear explosions that shook mountains and crumbled rocks.

Cesium (Cs) is one crazy element. It is a metal that melts in a warm room. Of course, you wouldn't want to be in a room with cesium, because it explodes if it touches air. You wouldn't want to be underwater with it because—yup—it explodes when it touches water. So what do you do with an element that explodes in air and water? Use it as a drilling fluid, of course. It is also used in building the atomic clock. Mixed with other elements that that stabilize it, cesium is used to make some of the most accurate clocks in the world.

When people think of explosions, they usually imagine a scientist in the lab sloshing chemicals from one beaker to another.

Hydrogen (H) is the most common element in the universe. When attached to oxygen molecules, it makes up water and hydrogen peroxide. But by itself, hydrogen is incredibly explosive. A single spark can cause pure hydrogen to erupt into flames. That's what happened to the Hindenburg.

In 1937, Germany was flying zeppelins filled with hydrogen. The gas is lighter than air and was used to float the gigantic balloons in the air, complete with passengers and flight crews. But a static spark ignited the hydrogen, and the Hindenburg exploded in flames, killing 36 people.

[Geologists have found evidence of spontaneously occurring nuclear explosions that shook mountains and crumbled rocks.]

Today blimps or zeppelins are filled with helium. Helium is also lighter than air, but it is not explosive.

STINK FOR SAFETY

Methane is a chemical that people use every day to heat their homes and cook their food. When it is controlled properly, methane is a valuable tool for civilization. But uncontrolled methane can erupt into a fireball that can blow up buildings in an instant. Naturally occurring methane is a colorless, odorless gas. That's a problem, because humans can't tell when there is too much methane in a room, and it's so explosive that turning on a light can set off an explosion. To protect people from the dangers of a methane explosion, gas companies add a sulphur, or slightly rotten egg, smell to the gas. That way people can tell when methane leaks into a room or building. They know to get out fast and call for help.

SHUTTLE EXPLOSION

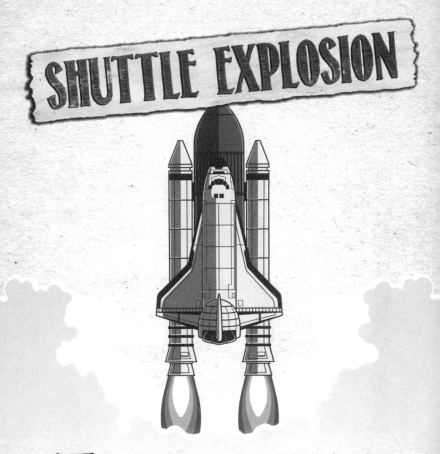

The *Challenger* shuttle was loaded and in place on the launch pad. The cold and sunny January morning in 1986 looked like the perfect day for a space launch. Crowds of people gathered around their televisions to watch the historic launch. This was one of the most exciting projects NASA had planned in years.

On board the shuttle was the very first civilian astronaut, teacher Christa McAuliffe. It was a grand experiment by NASA, who hoped that McAuliffe would help students across America gain a better understanding of space and the science involved. The teacher-astronaut was assigned several experiments to conduct, and she would also give the first science lessons broadcast from outer space. Classrooms across America were excited to be involved in the NASA space program.

Crowds of people gathered around their televisions to watch the historic launch. This was one of the most exciting projects NASA had planned in years.

At 11:38 a.m., the shuttle was cleared for launch. Engines roared and the shuttle shot up into the sky. Crowds cheered and clapped. This was the 10th trip for *Challenger*, and it would be a 6-day mission. Then the shuttle would return and be used again. The reusable shuttle was one of NASA's most successful projects.

But as people were watching the rocket soar up to the atmosphere, they suddenly saw fire and smoke surround the shuttle. The *Challenger* broke apart in midair—pieces fell to the ground and splashed into the ocean. Students in classrooms across America watched as the *Challenger* exploded on live television.

It was one of the worst disasters in the history of the space program. All seven astronauts on board were killed. Americans' faith in the space program was shaken. What could have happened to cause the shuttle to explode? What could they do to prevent another tragedy?

Scientists went to work trying to piece together the clues. Navy rescue teams scoured the ocean for debris from the shuttle. Everything that was found was brought back for the scientists to use in their investigations. Was there something wrong with the rocket booster? Had the math and physics calculations been wrong?

After months of investigations, scientists came to the conclusion that the deadly explosion had been caused by the failure of two rubber O-rings. These rings had been designed to separate the sections of the rocket booster. But the cold temperatures that morning had made the rubber rings brittle. Instead of keeping the sections separate, they broke apart, allowing burning gas to reach the rocket. It was a disaster that could have been prevented.

Scientist Richard Feynman was one of the people charged with investigating the *Challenger* disaster. He did a simple experiment with a small rubber O-ring. He submerged the ring in icy water and showed that when it was cold, the ring lost its flexibility. His experiment showed just how important it is to pay attention to every small detail in a project. Even the smallest thing can cause terrible problems.

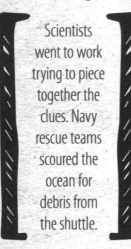

Scientists went to work trying to piece together the clues. Navy rescue teams scoured the ocean for debris from the shuttle.

It was almost 3 years before the United States launched another shuttle, but on September 29, 1988, the shuttle *Discovery* launched successfully and deployed a satellite. For the next 15 years, space shuttles flew without major problems, but in 2003 the *Columbia* space shuttle disintegrated as it re-entered Earth's atmosphere. Once again, the world remembered how dangerous space travel was and mourned the deaths of seven more crew members.

The reusable shuttle program flew missions for 30 years, giving scientists decades of new information about space and flight. In 2011, the program was officially retired. But new programs have been launched. Today NASA is developing the most advanced spacecraft ever invented. Called *Orion*, the spacecraft is designed to take four astronauts on missions beyond the moon. They plan to visit an asteroid and travel to Mars.

BLAST OFF

You can watch NASA test its newest rocket engine. Go to http://www.space.com/33292-nasa-test-fires-next-generation-rocket-engine.html.

The *Challenger* Crew

Science Lab

O-RING EXPERIMENT

ry an experiment similar to Dr. Feynman's O-ring test to understand why the *Challenger* O-rings failed.

MATERIALS

» Rubber O-ring (You can get these at hardware and auto parts stores, or someone in your family may have one in their repair supplies.)

» Glass of ice water

When you get the O-ring, take some time to play with it. Stretch it out. How does it feel at room temperature? Will it stretch and move easily? The O-rings on the space shuttle needed to be flexible, not stiff. If they got stiff, the seal would break and the shuttle would fail.

Now put the O-ring in the ice water for 2 minutes. After 2 minutes, pull it out and try to stretch it. What happens? Is it more or less flexible?

You should find that a cold O-ring is much harder to stretch. It becomes inflexible when it is too cold. This is what happened on the *Challenger*. The rings got too cold, and the seal broke.

Science Lab

WATER BOTTLE ROCKET

You can study the effects of air and water pressure by creating a water bottle rocket. It's easy and explosive fun. You will need a large outdoor area for this experiment, plus an adult helper.

MATERIALS

- » An empty 2-liter soda bottle
- » Bicycle pump with Schrader needle (the kind used to air up basketballs)
- » A wine bottle cork
- » Water
- » Empty 5-gallon bucket
- » Bath towels
- » Large darning needle

Take the wine cork and stick it in the top of the soda bottle to make sure it fits snugly. If it is too large, have an adult carve it to the correct width. Then have an adult cut the cork in half so that it is shorter than the needle on your air pump. This is important, because the opening of the needle needs to be exposed and inserted into the bottle so it can work correctly.

Use the large needle to poke a hole through the center of the cork. This is where you will insert the air pump needle. Next, set the 5-gallon bucket in the center of an open yard or field. Put the towel inside the bucket. You will use the towel to help the bottle sit upright inside the bucket.

Next, pour two or three cups of water into the plastic bottle. Place the cork in the top of the bottle and insert the air pump needle into the cork. Have the needle attached to the air pump hose.

Carefully set the bottle in the bucket with the cork down. You can use the towel as padding to help the bottle stay upright. The hose will be attached to the pump sitting next to the bucket. Have an adult pump the bicycle pump until the rocket blows! The air pressure will push out the cork, and the bottle will take off!

Science Lab

FIREWORKS IN A JAR

 tarfish Prime put on a fireworks display in the sky. You can make a fireworks display in a jar.

MATERIALS

- » Clean, clear glass jar with a lid
- » Cooking oil
- » Food coloring
- » Water
- » Pie plate
- » Fork
- » Spatula

Fill the jar 3/4 of the way full with warm water. Place several dots of food coloring in the pie plate. You can use any colors you chose. Make at least 12 dots. Then add 4 tablespoons of cooking oil. Mix together with a fork. Use a spatula to scrape the oil and food coloring mixture into the jar of water. Then watch what happens inside the jar.

The food coloring will dissolve in water, but not in the oil. Because the oil is lighter or less dense than water, it will float at the top of the water and slowly release the drops of food coloring. The drops of food coloring look like they are exploding in the water, but they are actually dissolving, making a fireworks display.

Science Lab

BATHTUB BOMBS

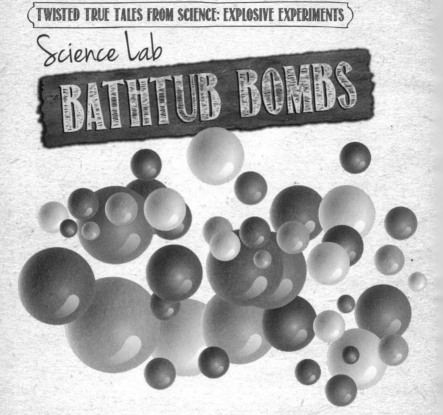

 t's time for an explosion—in your bathtub! It is pretty simple to make a bath bomb, but you do need some special ingredients.

MATERIALS

» 1 cup citric acid (you can buy this where you buy canning supplies)

» 1 cup baking soda

» 1/2 cup light cooking oil (olive oil, canola oil, etc.)

- » 1/2 cup cornstarch
- » Food coloring
- » Scented oil (can be purchased in drugstores or beauty departments)
- » Large bowl
- » 12-ounce drinking glass
- » Fork
- » Cookie sheet covered in wax paper

First, stir all of the dry ingredients together in the large bowl. Use a fork to make sure they are well mixed.

Pour the cooking oil into the glass and add a few drops of the scented oil. Stir it together. Then add a few drops of food coloring and stir until the oil is uniform in color.

Now pour the oil mixture into the bowl of dry ingredients and mix until it is evenly moist. Use your hands to shape the mix into mounds the size of your palm. Place each mound on the cookie sheet and let it dry overnight.

Once the bombs are dry, you can use them in the tub. Bombs away!

NEW
DEVELOPMENTS

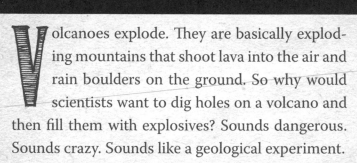

iMUSH

Volcanoes explode. They are basically exploding mountains that shoot lava into the air and rain boulders on the ground. So why would scientists want to dig holes on a volcano and then fill them with explosives? Sounds dangerous. Sounds crazy. Sounds like a geological experiment.

Ever since Mount St. Helens erupted in 1980, scientists have been trying to learn more about how the volcano works and what causes the eruptions. When the side blew off the volcano located in the state of Washington, it sent an eruption column 15 miles in the air. It melted glaciers, caused gigantic mudslides, and created the largest landslide ever recorded. The blast killed 58 people and thousands of wild animals. It leveled 200 houses and 47 bridges, and destroyed 185 miles of highway.

Volcanoes explode. They are basically exploding mountains that shoot lava into the air and rain boulders on the ground.

Government researchers, scientists, and public safety officials have all called for more research into the volcano in the hope of being able to predict the next major eruption. Lives depend on early warning, and Mount St. Helens continues to spew gas and lava. It had small eruptions in both 2004 and 2008. Predicting the next eruption is critical.

In 2014, scientists came up with a new idea for how to learn about what is going on in the layers of rock deep beneath the volcano. They named the program iMUSH (Imaging Magma Under St. Helens). They began drilling 80-foot-deep wells all around the mountain and filling them with explosives. Then they used the help of volunteers to cover the mountain with thousands of portable seismometers. Seismometers are used to measure the strength of the Earth's movements during earthquakes or volcanic eruptions. People went in to the mountains and forests of Mount St. Helens on foot, horseback, and in four-wheel drive vehicles to place the seismometers in every remote location.

When the seismometers were in place and dozens of wells had been drilled and set with explosives, the experiments began. Researchers set off the explosions and measured the results of the blasts. The data they recorded helped scientists to determine what the ground under Mount St. Helens looks like and how the magma may flow. Knowing how the Earth moves and shifts under the volcano can give scientists clues as to when the volcano may explode again.

BIGGEST EXPLOSION IN THE UNIVERSE

stronomers in Australia never expected to find a gigantic explosion in outer space. But in 2007, the CSIRO Parkes Observatory radio telescope in New South Wales detected an explosion so huge that it gave off more energy in a millisecond than the sun does in 10,000 years.

The astronomers were astonished. What could cause an explosion so huge? Where did it come from? And would there be more?

But in 2007, the CSIRO Parkes Observatory radio telescope in New South Wales detected an explosion so huge that it gave off more energy in a millisecond than the sun does in 10,000 years.

A team of international scientists set out on a 4-year search of the skies to see if they could find another massive explosion. They used the 210-foot radio telescope to focus, or stare at, different regions of the sky. It took months of investigation, but finally they found another massive explosion just like the first one. In all, they found 16 enormous explosions that they could not explain.

Scientists call the explosions FRBs, or Fast Radio Bursts. The explosions are incredibly bright and short. Most explosions that happen in space can be observed over days or even months, but the FRBs happen in milliseconds. Because they are so bright, the astronomers have been able to learn that they did not come from our own galaxy. They originate somewhere outside of the Milky Way.

So what causes the gigantic explosions? Scientists still aren't sure. They may be caused when a neutron star orbits a supernova. (A supernova is a star that suddenly gets really bright and then explodes.) The explosion of the supernova would be even bigger because of the reaction with the neutron star's magnetic field.

Or it could be caused by a huge burst of energy from a magnetar. A magnetar is a special kind of neutron star. (A neutron star is a dead star that is packed full of neutrons.) Magnetars have crazy strong magnetic fields. Their magnetic field is a quadrillion times stronger than the Earth's. The magnetic field is so strong that if a human got within 600 miles of one, he or she would simply dissolve.

All of his or her atoms would just break apart. It is entirely possible that these strange stars give off the FRBs.

Physicists have done calculations, and they estimate that these explosions happen somewhere in space every 10 seconds. That's right—colossal explosions happen in space every 10 seconds. Better than a fireworks show! Even though the immense explosions are frequent, they have a short signal duration, and that makes them hard to find.

Astronomers still have more questions than they have answers about the FRB explosions, but in the spring of 2015, they got one major answer. They were monitoring the skies for FRBs and had a plan in place that as soon as one was detected, there would be an immediate search for any remaining traces of the explosion. On April 18, the astronomers saw a blip that indicated an FRB. Immediately, telescopes around the world turned to look at that part of the sky. Two hours later, an Australian telescope had spotted the afterglow of an explosion. They were able to track the FRB to an older galaxy that is 6 billion light years away from the Milky Way.

Lucky for Earth, the explosions are a very long way away and are no threat to our galaxy. But the strange FRBs are still under investigation. Scientists still want to know exactly what causes them, and they hope that as they study the biggest explosions in the universe, they may learn about some other mysteries, like what makes dark matter and if it is related to even bigger explosions. Scientists are still scanning the skies looking for the next great explosion.

EXPLODING PARTICLES AND BLACK HOLES

People warned scientists not to build it. They were afraid that the huge machine might explode and create a black hole that could swallow the Earth. Protestors filed lawsuits, staged demonstrations, and even set up a Facebook page: "People against the Large Hadron Collider." But the scientists built it anyway.

It is called the Large Hadron Collider, and it's not just large—it's ginormous! Buried 574 feet deep, in a tunnel near Geneva, Switerzland, the LHC machine is 17 miles in circumfer-ence. That's the size of six Indy 500 racetracks! Inside the accelerator, a powerful system of magnets makes parts of atoms, called *hadrons*, fly around the track at the speed of light. The hadrons are forced to go in opposite directions, and then they smash together in what looks like a huge explosion. As the hadrons collide, they smash apart just like they would if they were exploding, but it is caused by a collision.

Protestors filed lawsuits, staged demonstrations, and even set up a Facebook page: "People against the Large Hadron Collider." But the scientists built it anyway.

Scientists use detectors to learn how the parti-cles interact. It takes 3,000 computers to compute all the data generated by the LHC collisions. When the hadrons smash together, they get super hot. For a few seconds, the energy they release is 100,000 times hotter than the sun.

Physicists are exploding these hadrons in the hopes of learning more about the structure of space and time. They are trying to replicate the conditions of the universe just seconds after it was created. They believe that this will give them information on some of the more mysterious parts of the universe, such as dark matter, black holes, exotic particles, and rainbow universes.

SEE THE LHC

You can take a video tour of the Large Hadron Collider at https://www.youtube.com/watch?v=UI98Cj29hK4.

HOT STUFF

The Large Hadron Collider set the record for the hottest man-made temperature on Earth. In 2012, the LHC recorded temperatures of 4 TRILLION degrees Celsius. That's hotter than the surface of the sun!

Because it generates such high temperatures, it must be cooled. Part of the Large Hadron Collider is a refrigerator big enough to hold 150,000 sausages and colder than deep outer space.

The LHC breaks all kinds of records, not just the hot ones. The combined strands of the superconducting cable in the LHC could wrap around the Earth's equator almost seven times. If all of the filaments of the strands were laid end to end, they would stretch to the sun and back five times with enough left over to wrap around the moon!

QUEEN OF EXPLOSIONS

It's called a *thermobaric weapon*, and it is one of the deadliest bombs in the U.S. artillery. When this bomb explodes, it sucks in oxygen from the air to make a high temperature explosion. The resulting fireball uses up all the oxygen in the blast area. Buildings and people are disintegrated. This explosive weapon was invented by Nguyet Anh Duong and her team of scientists at the Department of Defense.

Now known as the Queen of Bombs, Duong grew up in Vietnam during the 1960s at the height of the Vietnam War. She lived through bombings, food shortages, and in daily fear of the invading North Vietnamese Army. Her family worked together to survive until the horrible day in 1975, when the Communist tanks rolled into Saigon. Her parents decided it was time to get out of Vietnam.

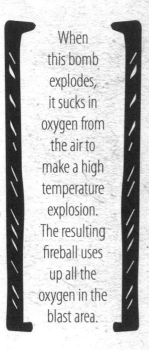

When this bomb explodes, it sucks in oxygen from the air to make a high temperature explosion. The resulting fireball uses up all the oxygen in the blast area.

They had to leave their home, friends, family, and all their possessions behind.

Duong and her parents joined hundreds of other South Vietnamese who crowded onto tiny boats and launched themselves into the South China Sea. Their one hope was to find a ship that would rescue them and take them to a refugee camp. Bobbing in the sea, Duong's tiny boat was spotted by a South Vietnamese ship. Duong remembers having to balance on the small boat, the waves rocking her back and forth, and make a giant leap across the water to the larger ship. Relief flooded her mind as she landed on the deck of the larger ship. Now she would have a chance at freedom.

When her family arrived in the United States, Duong did not know English, but by the end of her first year of American high school, she was one of the top students. She loved science and thought about studying to be a doctor, but found out that dissecting animals made her feel sick. She liked math and chemistry and earned college degrees in both chemical engineering and computer science. Then she thought about what she wanted to do with the rest of her life.

Duong loved her adopted home and wanted to serve the United States. She went to work for the Department of Defense, hoping that with her work she could pay back the soldiers and people who had helped her family. She began working on "things that go swish and boom"—rockets and the explosives they carry.

When she was assigned to develop a special missile to help in the War on Terror, Duong and her team designed a new type of bomb. It was a thermobaric explosive. This bomb was different from regular bombs that do their job by punching through things with the force of their exploding fragments, or blasting and collapsing things. Her bomb was designed to detonate slowly so that the bomb could bore deep underground or into caves before it exploded. It was designed to be used in Afghanistan, where many of the enemy combatants hid in caves or underground bunkers.

Some people have criticized Duong for building such destructive weapons, but she argues that the weapons that her team creates are actually designed to work smartly to take out the enemies of the United States and cause as little collateral damage as possible. If there has to be war, Duong says she wants to protect as many people as she can.

FIFTH-GRADE SCIENTIST

Legend:
- ■ OXYGEN
- ■ NITROGEN
- ■ CARBON

TETRANITRATOXYCARBON

In the winter of 2012, Clara Lazen was busy working on her fifth-grade science assignment. Her teacher, Mr. Boehr, had talked to the class about how chemicals are made up of different elemental atoms. Then he gave the students sets of atom models. Their assignment was to put together the atoms and create a molecule.

Clara took the springs and balls and arranged them in different ways. She knew that a model of a stable chemical had to have all the holes filled and connect together. She fiddled and worked with the atoms until she built some-

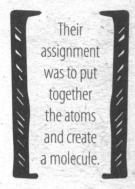

Their assignment was to put together the atoms and create a molecule.

thing that looked like it was balanced and fit well. Then she showed it to Mr. Boehr and asked if she had built a model of a real chemical compound.

Mr. Boehr looked closely at the model. It seemed like it could be a real chemical compound, but it wasn't something he recognized. Mr. Boehr took a picture of the molecule and sent it to a friend of his who was a chemistry professor at Humboldt State University.

Professor Zoellner was stumped. It looked like the atoms were connected correctly, but he had never seen a molecule like this before. He ran it through a computer database and found that 10-year-old Clara had just discovered a new molecule. And it wasn't just any mole-

Clara Lazen, 2012

cule: This was a molecule that had the potential to store energy and create huge explosions.

The molecule consisted of oxygen, nitrogen, and carbon with a molecular structure similar to nitroglycerine. They named the new molecule Tetranitratoxycarbon. Clara became one of the youngest people in the world to discover a new explosive molecule. Scientists are now working to see if they can synthesize the actual molecule and make it in a laboratory. If they can, it may prove to be more powerful than nitroglycerine.

Clara became one of the youngest people in the world to discover a new explosive molecule.

Science Lab

SOAP ERUPTION

olcanoes erupt with magma from the forces of underground gasses and pressure. You can make your own eruption with the help of a microwave.

MATERIALS

- » An adult helper
- » Bar of Ivory soap
- » Microwave

With the help of an adult, place the bar of Ivory soap in the microwave. Set the microwave on high and let it run for 2 minutes. Watch and see what happens to the Ivory soap. As the molecules of air trapped inside the Ivory soap are heated up, they expand. This pressure causes the soap to expand or erupt—similar to heated magma.

Science Lab

GEYSER ERUPTION

The forces of shifting continental plates and heated gasses inside the Earth often cause water geysers to erupt like those found in volcanic areas.

You can create your own geyser with some candy and a bottle of Diet Coke. This is a messy experiment, so you will want to do this outside.

MATERIALS

» 2-liter bottle of Diet Coke

» Half a pack of Mentos candy

Stand the soda bottle upright on a flat surface. Unscrew the lid and drop three or four Mentos in the bottle, and then RUN! It will cause an eruption of soda from the bottle. The carbon dioxide gas that is in the soda is reacting with the surface of the Mentos candy to cause this eruption.

POP GOES THE GEYSER

To see a video of a geyser as it progressively explodes, check out this video of the Beehive Geyser in Yellowstone National Park: https://www.youtube.com/watch?v=y8gLhHzPY5M.

Science Lab

FOAMPLOSION

Safe explosions can be fun and foamy. Try this explosion to see what happens when you mix hydrogen peroxide and a microscopic fungus called *yeast*.

MATERIALS

- » 1-liter plastic bottle
- » Small plastic or paper cup
- » Funnel
- » At least 4 ounces (120ml) hydrogen peroxide
- » Liquid dishwashing soap
- » Food coloring
- » 1 package dry yeast
- » 4 tablespoon of warm water

Use the funnel to pour the hydrogen peroxide into the liter plastic bottle. Add a good squirt of dish soap to the hydrogen peroxide and three drops of food coloring. Swish the ingredients together in the bottle so they are mixed.

Next, pour four tablespoons of warm tap water into the small cup. Then add the whole package of yeast to the water. Use a spoon to stir it together. If your yeast mixture is too thick and feels like paste, add a little more water. The mixture should be a little runny so it can be poured.

Now get ready for a foamplosion! Pour the yeast mix into the plastic bottle and see what happens. Be patient. It could take a few seconds to explode, but when it does—you'll be amazed!

The explosion is made because the yeast reacts with the hydrogen peroxide and releases its oxygen molecules. This is an exothermic reaction and gives off heat. Feel the plastic bottle. It will feel warm. The foam is safe to touch and can be washed down the drain or put in the trash.

BIBLIOGRAPHY

BOOKS

Breuer, W. B. (2000). *Secret weapons of WWII.* New York, NY: Castle Books.

Brown, S. R. (2005). *A most damnable invention: Dynamite, nitrates, and the making of the modern world.* New York, NY: Thomas Dunne Books.

Hayes, W. (2011). *What went wrong: Investigating the worst man-made and natural disasters.* New York, NY: Hearst Books.

James, P., & Thorpe, N. (1994). *Ancient inventions.* New York, NY: Ballantine Books.

Kelly, J. (2004). *Gunpowder: Alchemy, bombards, and pyrotechnics: The history of the explosive that changed the world.* New York, NY: Basic Books.

Withington, J. (2010). *Disaster!: A history of earthquakes, floods, plagues, and other catastrophes.* New York, NY: Skyhorse Publishing.

WEBSITES

American Oil & Gas Historical Society. (n.d.). *New London School explosion.* Retrieved from http://aoghs.org/oil-almanac/new-london-texas-school-explosion

Anderson, L. (2012). *The man who didn't like his obituary.* Retrieved from http://www.liveyour magic.com/2012/03/the-man-who-didnt-like-his-obituary

BBC News. (2016). *Chernobyl disaster: Ukraine marks 30th anniversary*. Retrieved from http://www.bbc.com/news/world-europe-36136286

Block, M. (2006). 'Voices from Chernobyl': Survivors' stories. *NPR*. Retrieved from http://www.npr.org/2006/04/21/5355810/voices-of-chernobyl-survivors-stories

Broken arrows: Nuclear weapons accidents. (n.d.). Retrieved from http://www.atomicarchive.com/Almanac/Brokenarrows_static.shtml

CERN. (n.d.). *The Large Hadron Collider*. Retrieved from https://home.cern/topics/large-hadron-collider

Famous Scientists. (2014). *Luis Alvarez*. Retrieved from http://www.famousscientists.org/luis-alvarez

Famous Scientists. (2014). *Robert Bunsen*. Retrieved from http://www.famousscientists.org/robert-bunsen

The fire beater. (1953, February 9). [Article from *TIME Magazine*.] Retrieved from http://facsimilemagazine.com/2010/06/#firebeater

Fireworks in a jar. (2012). Retrieved from http://stem-works.com/external/activity/556

Golgowski, N. (2012). Ten-year-old discovers 'new molecule' while tinkering with education model. *DailyMail.com.* Retrieved from http://www.dailymail.co.uk/news/article-2096481/Ten-year-old-discovers-new-molecule-tinkering-educational-model.html

Grossman, D. (2009). *Graf Zeppelin history.* Retrieved from http://www.airships.net/lz127-graf-zeppelin/history

Growing a Jeweled Rose. (n.d.). *Exploding art—Paint bags.* Retrieved from http://www.growing ajeweledrose.com/2013/04/paintbombs.html

Gunpowder and firearms. (n.d.). Retrieved from http://depts.washington.edu/chinaciv/miltech/firearms.htm

Hammock Boy. (n.d.). *2 liter rocket.* Retrieved from http://www.instructables.com/id/2-Liter-Rocket

Havely, J. (2003). China's Ming dynasty astronaut. *CNN.* Retrieved from http://edition.cnn.com/2003/TECH/space/09/30/china.wanhu

Holman, B. (2015). Why we should remember the first world war's female munitions workers. *The Guardian.* Retrieved from https://www.theguardian.com/society/2015/jan/06/girls-stirred-devils-porridge-first-world-war-remember-munitions-workers

How does blowout control work? (n.d.). Retrieved from http://www.rigzone.com/training/insight_pf.asp?i_id=300

Imaging magma under St. Helens. (n.d.). Retrieved from http://imush.org

John, S. (n.d.). *The top 5 most explosive elements on Earth.* Retrieved from http://science-facts.top5.com/the-top-5-most-explosive-elements-on-earth

King, G. (2012). Going nuclear over the Pacific. *Smithsonian.com.* Retrieved from http://www.smithsonianmag.com/history/going-nuclear-over-the-pacific-24428997

Klein, C. (2012). The Hindenburg disaster: 9 surprising facts. *History.com.* Retrieved from http://www.history.com/news/the-hindenburg-disaster-9-surprising-facts

Lam, A. (n.d.). *Bomb lady: Vietnamese American makes tools for War on Terror.* Retrieved from http://www.vietamericanvets.com/Page-Diaspora-BombLady.htm

La Vone, M. (2014). The space shuttle Challenger disaster. *Space Safety Magazine.* Retrieved from http://www.spacesafetymagazine.com/space-disasters/challenger-disaster

Morris, H. (2004). *LHC Machine outreach: Interesting facts.* Retrieved from http://lhc-machine-out reach.web.cern.ch/lhc-machine-outreach/lhc-interesting-facts.htm

The National Security Archive. (2015). *The atomic bomb and the end of World War II.* Retrieved from http://nsarchive.gwu.edu/NSAEBB/NSA EBB162/index.htm

NobelPrize.org. (2017). *All Nobel Prizes.* Retrieved from http://www.nobelprize.org/nobel_prizes/lists/all/

NNDB. (2015). *Robert Wilhelm Bunsen.* Retrieved from http://www.nndb.com/people/900/00009 5615

Nuclear Energy Institute. (2016). *World statistics: Nuclear energy around the world.* Retrieved from http://www.nei.org/Knowledge-Center/Nuclear-Statistics/World-Statistics

Plait, P. (2012). The 50th anniversary of Starfish Prime: The nuke that shook the world. *Discover Magazine.* Retrieved from http://blogs.discovermagazine.com/badastronomy/2012/07/09/the-50th-anniversary-of-starfish-prime-the-nuke-that-shook-the-world/#.V0SY NY-cHeJ

Redd, N. T. (2013). Mysterious deep-space explosions baffle scientists. *Space.com*. Retrieved from http://www.space.com/21861-deep-space-radio-explosions-mystery.html

Redd, N. T. (2016). Dark matter clue: Strange radio bursts finally reveal host galaxy. *Space.com*. Retrieved from http://www.space.com/32055-mystery-fast-radio-burst-space-explosions-location.html

Ringertz, N. (2014). Alfred Nobel—his life and work. *Nobelprize.org*. Retrieved from http://www.nobelprize.org/alfred_nobel/biographical/articles/life-work

Science Kids. (n.d.). *Diet Coke and Mentos eruption*. Retrieved from http://www.sciencekids.co.nz/experiments/dietcokementos.html

Sciencebob.com. (n.d.). *Eggshell geode crystals*. Retrieved from https://sciencebob.com/eggshell-geode-crystals

The Scotsman. (2005). *Devil's porridge: How world's largest factory helped win The Great War*. Retrieved from http://www.scotsman.com/lifestyle/devil-s-porridge-how-world-s-largest-factory-helped-win-the-great-war-1-465872

Sheakoski, M. (2014). *Exploding baggie science experiment.* Retrieved from http://www.coffee cupsandcrayons.com/exploding-baggie-science-experiment

Shellman, M. (2015). "MAC"—A tribute to the "father" of oil well firefighting. *Oilpro.com.* Retrieved from http://oilpro.com/post/19281/mac-a-tribute-to-the-father-of-oil-well-fire fighting

Singh, T. (2012). 10-year-old discovers new molecule that could help improve energy storage. *inhabit.com.* Retrieved from http://inhabitat.com/10-year-old-girl-discovers-new-molecule-that-could-help-energy-storage

Steve Spangler Science. (n.d.). *Kid-friendly exploding toothpaste.* Retrieved from http://www.stevespanglerscience.com/lab/experiments/elephants-toothpaste/#experiment-procedure

Steve Spangler Science. (n.d.). *Soap soufflé.* Retrieved from http://www.stevespanglerscience.com/lab/experiments/soap-souffle

Tarantola, A. (2013). The biggest bomb in the history of the world. *Gizmodo.com.* Retrieved from http://gizmodo.com/5977824/the-biggest-bomb-in-the-history-of-the-world

Ulberg, C. (2015). iMUSH: Imaging Magma Under St. Helens. *GeoPRISMS*. http://geoprisms.org/education/report-from-the-field/imush-spring 2015

Vowles, A. (2013). Homemade bath bombs for kids. *All Parenting*. Retrieved from http://www.allparenting.com/my-family/articles/966665/homemade-bath-bombs-for-kids

Wellerstein, A. (2016). The demon core and the strange death of Louis Slotin. *The New Yorker.* http://www.newyorker.com/tech/elements/demon-core-the-strange-death-of-louis-slotin

Wikipedia. (n.d.). *Gunpowder*. Retrieved from https://en.wikipedia.org/wiki/Gunpowder

Wikipedia. (n.d.). *History of cannon*. https://en.wikipedia.org/wiki/History_of_cannon

Wikipedia. (n.d.). *Large Hadron Collider*. https://en.wikipedia.org/wiki/Large_Hadron_Collider

Will, G. F. (2007). Anh Duong, out of debt. *Newsweek.* Retrieved from http://www.newsweek.com/anh-duong-out-debt-94755

Zeilig, M. (1995). *Louis Slotin and 'the invisible killer.'* Retrieved from http://web.ncf.ca/lavitt/louisslotin/beaver.html

ABOUT THE AUTHOR

Stephanie Bearce is a writer, teacher, and science nerd. She likes teaching kids how to blow up toothpaste and dissect worms. She also loves collecting rocks and keeps a huge collection of fossilized bones in her basement. When she is not exploding experiments in her kitchen or researching strange science facts in the library, Stephanie likes to explore catacombs and museums with her husband, Darrell.

MORE TWISTED TRUE TALES FROM SCIENCE

Twisted True Tales From Science: Disaster Discoveries
ISBN: 978-1-61821-574-1

London was once covered in a fog so polluted that it killed 12,000 people. The Aleppo earthquake killed 230,000 people, and a wall of water mysteriously wiped out the whole town of Burnham-on-Sea. All of these were catastrophic disasters, but they led to important discoveries in science. Learn about how the earth turned to liquid in New Zealand and what happens when a tsunami meets a nuclear reactor. These stories may sound twisted and strange, but they are all true tales from science!

MORE TWISTED TRUE TALES FROM SCIENCE

Twisted True Tales From Science: Insane Inventors

ISBN: 978-1-61821-570-3

Nikola Tesla was crazy smart. He invented the idea for cell phones in 1893, discovered alternating current, and invented a death ray gun. Of course, he also talked to pigeons, ate only boiled food, and was scared of women who wore jewelry. He was an insane inventor. So was Henry Cavendish, who discovered hydrogen, calculated the density of the Earth, and was so scared of people that he had to write notes to communicate. Sir Isaac Newton discovered the laws of gravity, believed in magic, and thought he could make a potion to create gold. These stories may sound twisted, but they're all true tales from science!

Twisted True Tales From Science: Medical Mayhem

ISBN: 978-1-61821-572-7

Ground-up mummy bones, leeches sucking human blood, and a breakfast of dried mouse paste. It sounds like a horror movie, but those were actual medicines prescribed by early doctors. Medical students studied anatomy on bodies stolen from graves and had to operate on people while they were awake. Learn about the medicines that came from poison and doctors who experimented on themselves and their families. It's a twisted tale of medical mayhem, but it's all true!